VOCABULARY
CONNECTIONS

Book I
General Words

VOCABULARY CONNECTIONS

Book I
General Words

Marianne C. Reynolds
Mercer County Community College

Boston, Massachusetts   Burr Ridge, Illinois   Dubuque, Iowa
Madison, Wisconsin   New York, New York   San Francisco, California   St. Louis, Missouri

McGraw-Hill

A Division of The **McGraw·Hill** *Companies*

VOCABULARY CONNECTIONS: BOOK I GENERAL WORDS

This book is printed on acid-free paper.

4567890 DOC/DOC 09876543

ISBN 0-07-052628-1

Vice president and editorial director: *Phil Butcher*
Sponsoring editor: *Sarah Moyers*
Marketing manager: *Lesley Denton*
Project manager: *Lynne Basler*
Production supervisor: *Karen Thigpen*
Senior designer: *Laurie J. Entringer*
Compositor: *Electronic Publishing Services, Inc.*
Typeface: *10/12 Palatino*
Printer: *R. R. Donnelley & Sons—Crawfordsville*

http://www.mhcollege.com

For Roland, Candy, Julia,
Chris, and all my other students
who helped me develop and try
out the exercises in this book

PREFACE

Many people would like to have a larger vocabulary. If you check the "self-help" section of a bookstore, you may find several books devoted to helping people learn new words. As with many other subjects, though, vocabulary is hard to learn on your own. Most of us benefit from the discipline and schedule a course provides that independent study does not. In addition to the advantage of studying vocabulary in a college course, you have the benefit of exposure to a variety of words in your other courses and academic activities. The business you are in as a college student is "word dependent." In your classes and your studies, you are constantly bombarded with words. You hear them; you see them; you write them. If you make a conscious effort to learn and remember the meanings of new words, you will find your "environment of words" a great help.

We can expand our vocabulary in several ways. As children, part of our normal development is language acquisition. For young children learning to speak, the rate of new words learned is phenomenal. They usually begin to use new words as labels for familiar people (*Mommy*) or objects (*cookie*). Adults who learn a new language also may begin by asking the names of objects: "What is this called?" or "How do you say *casa* [house] in English?" For both groups, this language learning is an exciting and rewarding process. Those of you who begin to work or study in a new field will also be exposed to a new vocabulary. A student who began a new job in a warehouse learned the term *palletizing*. Computer science students may learn a new meaning for the word *bursting*, as it applies to paper instead of balloons.

As a college student, your vocabulary development may not be as dramatic as that of a young child or a non-native speaker. But you will learn new words as you read and listen. Your professors may use words with which you are unfamiliar, and you may find new words in your textbooks and course-related reading. In many cases, these words will be the same, and the more often you meet them, the more likely you will learn and remember their meanings. A conscious effort on your part will make learning vocabulary easier. You may even enjoy it!

Learn to look for clues as you hear or read an unfamiliar word. In class, your professor may spontaneously provide a definition, or a student may ask for one. You may be able to tell the word's meaning from the context, the way it is used. The speaker's gestures, tone of voice, or the spelling of the word on the board may help as well. In print, you can use the context, a supplied definition, a glossary, or your dictionary as aids.

If you had the luxury of unlimited time to expand your vocabulary, you could probably rely solely on your exposure to new words, terms, and phrases. To be a successful college learner, though, you should probably make a more deliberate effort to learn most of the words you will meet in college situations. The English language is rich with synonyms, allowing readers and speakers to select words that clearly and specifically communicate their meanings. As a reader and listener, you will learn the meanings of many words that can be used interchangeably. Although it is admirable if you choose to incorporate many of the words you learn this semester into your speaking and writing vocabulary, your primary goal this semester should be recognition. When you complete the work in this textbook, you still may not be able to write from memory all the definitions you learned. If you learned them well, however, when you first studied them, you should be able to recall their meanings when you meet them in context in the future.

The texts in this series are designed to be practical. The three books can be used in any order. In fact, the order of the chapters within each book can be changed as well.

The first book deals with general vocabulary. Many college professors claim that they can teach their students the course-related terminology, but they also expect them to be knowledgeable about general, frequently used, college-level words. In this book, you will learn many words that can neither be defined by their word parts nor associated with a particular field. They are words that will come up in lectures, textbooks, newspaper and journal articles, and conversation among educated people. They were selected from high-frequency word lists, so you know you can count on seeing them again. Many instructors choose to begin with this book and teach the word parts and academic words later in the semester.

The second book concentrates on word parts—prefixes, suffixes, and roots. You will learn the meanings of the word parts and many words they make up. You may begin to think of words as puzzles. You can analyze words by identifying their parts to discover their meanings. You can also synthesize the word parts by putting them together to make new words. Learning word parts is a very efficient way to increase your vocabulary. There are so many English words that can be defined if you know the meanings of their parts. The benefits of your study time will be multiplied as you are able to unlock the meanings of a tremendous number of words. You will also find yourself using word parts of words you already know to help define new ones.

The third book presents words in academic context. College students take reading or first-year experience courses to help them do well in their college course work. The most practical way to teach you how to define unfamiliar words when you meet them in your textbooks is to give you some samples. The subject fields are representative of courses most college students take during their first or second year. Certainly you won't learn all the vocabulary you need for your psychology or biology course in a chapter. But you will learn some key terms in each field and practice using textbook material to define them. You may also be surprised at how many of these terms are defined in the text and how many others' meanings you can figure out.

In addition to working through the exercises in this book and studying for the quizzes and tests, you may want to keep a personal journal. Some students find it beneficial to keep a record of unfamiliar words they meet on a daily basis. A note indicating the word, where you encountered it, and a brief definition is all that is necessary. Many of my students report that they find themselves recording the same word several times until they learn it. This experience shows the need to study as well as to write down unfamiliar words. It also supports the notion that some words occur more frequently than others and recommends their mastery. Research has shown that recreational or "free" reading also increases vocabulary development. Many college students complain that they barely have time to complete their course-related reading. Nevertheless, those who devote 20 minutes a day to reading for pleasure (a newspaper, magazine, novel, or nonfiction book) report a gain in word knowledge as well as other benefits.

Study often. Brief daily study sessions are better than a long cramming session just before a test. Study with classmates, discuss the meanings of the words, and make them your own. Tell someone who is curious about words an interesting new term you have learned. Ask someone to quiz you on the word meanings. Try to use one new word a day in your conversation or writing. Pay attention to words and don't be afraid to try them out. You may be surprised at the number of people who are interested in the origins of words and their meanings.

Marianne C. Reynolds

CONTENTS

Book I

INTRODUCTION

There are many general words whose meanings college students should know. Professors often complain that their unsuccessful students are deficient in their knowledge of general vocabulary. Even if they study and learn the technical terms, they have difficulty with the larger context of language. Students often complain that English has too many words that mean the same thing. They question the value of so many synonyms that they may never use in ordinary conversation. Indeed, there is a vast difference between the vocabulary needed to be a competent conversationalist and the vocabulary necessary to be a successful college reader. Researchers have investigated word usage in an effort to determine the most frequently used words. As you can imagine, words like *the, is,* and *he* are found at the top of the list. A study by Hartvig Dahl compared word usage in spoken English to the findings of Kucera and Francis regarding written material. (See the Bibliography at the back of the book for full references to these books.) He found that 848 words account for 90 percent of spoken usage, but nearly 8,000 words are required to account for 90 percent of written language. Those of you who feel more comfortable and competent in lecture and discussion sessions than in reading your textbooks may partially attribute that feeling to the difference in vocabulary requirements.

The words selected for study in this section of the text come from the Kucera/Francis analysis. In 1963–64, a group of written materials was selected to form the "Brown University Corpus." Five hundred samples of approximately 2,000 words each, representing 15 genres, were selected from adult reading material. The words included in these works were counted and ranked according to how often they appeared. In 1982, the words were re-ranked to correct some duplication errors in the original study. Over 50,000 words appeared, the most frequent of which are very familiar to most adults. All the words you will study in this section appeared frequently in the Brown corpus, so you can expect to meet them in your reading as well.

The last two chapters in this book deal with idioms, expressions that have a figurative rather than a literal meaning. Most of the idioms that are included are fairly common and have multiple meanings according to the context.

PRONUNCIATION KEY

Use the following simple pronunciation guide to help you pronounce the words you will study. A sample word is provided for each vowel symbol that is used in the word lists.

	Short Vowels (indicated with no mark)		*Long Vowels* (indicated with a straight line called a macron above the letter)
a	hat	ā	say, hate
e	bet	ē	me, seat
i	tin	ī	fine, sky
o	pot	ō	so, rode
u	cut	ū	mule, use

The schwa (ə) is a very common sound in the English language. It has the sound of "uh" and can be made by any vowel. Examples follow:

a	in above	(ə buv′)
e	in system	(sis′ təm)
u	in circus	(sûr′ kəs)

The doubled oo takes on a short or long sound, too.

Short		*Long*	
oo	cook	o͞o	boot

Additional Vowel Sounds

ä	father	ô	order, raw
â	air	û	term, urge

SECTION
ONE

HIGH-FREQUENCY WORDS

CHAPTER 1

In this chapter and the next seven, you will study general, high-frequency words that you can expect to encounter in your academic and recreational reading. Most cannot easily be defined by a knowledge of word parts, nor are they tied to a particular field of study. Since you will meet these words in textual reading situations, they are first presented here in context. You will be asked first to write a definition of the word according to how it is used in the sentence and passage. Then you will complete a matching exercise that will help you confirm your conclusions about the word's meanings. You can then review the word list, which gives dictionary-type definitions. Finally, you will complete more practice exercises to help you learn the words.

Read the following passage through completely. Then return to the beginning and write your definition for each numbered and underlined word.

New Ideas for Old Cities

Many cities in the United States have experienced a decline in prosperity and attractiveness as residents and businesses move out to the suburbs. (1) <u>Frequently</u>, a group of civic-minded citizens comes forward to try to preserve some of the city's former grandeur. In Georgia, for example, the Historic Savannah Foundation was (2) <u>established</u> in the 1950s to preserve and restore some of the city's old buildings that had fallen into disrepair. Some members of the committee were asked to (3) <u>determine</u> when an old house was about to be demolished. Since the group had no (4) <u>capital</u> at the beginning, all it could do was try to persuade someone to buy the property and restore it. The members quickly realized that, in order to make a (5) <u>significant</u> impact on preservation, they had to raise funds to buy the properties. A (6) <u>campaign</u> among the members raised the money to buy their first house. This marked the beginning of the (7) <u>effective</u> use of a revolving fund. The foundation would buy a property and resell it to someone who (8) <u>indicated</u> his or her intention to restore it. One of the (9) <u>requirements</u> was that restoration had to begin within 18 months of the purchase. After each house was sold, sometimes at a loss, the money was used again to buy another property. After several houses were beautifully restored and occupied, (10) <u>circumstances</u> for expanding the project became more favorable. Now the city can enjoy a historically preserved area that had been in decline, and the availability of attractive housing within the downtown area has increased.

Exercise 1: Define

Write your definition for each word as it is used in the passage.

1. frequently   *often*
2. established   *found; set up*
3. determine   *to conclude; find out*
4. capital   *money, fund*
5. significant   *important*
6. campaign   *special drive of project*

7. effective   _adequate, functioning_
8. indicated   _a sign, to showed_
9. requirements   _necessities_
10. circumstances   _condition_ .

Exercise 2: Match

Match the terms in Column A with their definitions in Column B.

Column A	*Column B*
1. campaign _g_	a. was a sign of; showed _8_
2. capital _d_	b. necessities _9_
3. circumstances _h_	c. often _6_
4. determine _i_	d. money; funds _2_
5. effective _j_	e. important; noticeable
6. established _f_	f. founded; set up
7. frequently _c_	g. a project or drive for _1_ a specific purpose
8. indicated _a_	h. conditions _3_
9. requirements _b_	i. to find out; to conclude
10. significant _e_	j. adequate; functioning

Exercise 3: Fill In

Fill in the letter of the word that best completes each sentence.

a. established   d. determine   g. significant   i. requirements
b. effective   e. frequently   h. circumstances   j. campaign
c. indicated   f. capital

_____ 1. One of the most _effective_ ways to combat poverty is through education.

_____ 2. In order to _determine_ class rank, counselors considered grades as well as the number and difficulty of the courses each student had completed.

_____ 3. An avid hockey fan, Ken _frequently_ attended New York Rangers' games as well as college games in the area.

_____ 4. Debbie's physician _stated_ complete bed rest for three weeks was the only way to recover her strength.

_____ 5. An underground student newspaper was _established_ to present alternative views to the more traditional approach of the official campus paper.

_____ 6. In spite of extremely difficult _____, Talomas managed to immigrate to the United States and earn a degree in computer science.

_____ 7. The United Way launched its _____ among area businesses and asked each employee to subscribe to a payroll deduction contribution.

_____ 8. Firefighters in some cities are being asked to complete medical training as one of the _requirements_ for employment.

_____ 9. A _significant_ difference exists between the lifetime earnings of high school and college graduates.

_____ 10. Without the _capital_ she borrowed from her relatives, Angelina would not have been able to open her catering business.

WORD LIST

The following list gives dictionary-type definitions of the words you are studying in this chapter. Each entry includes the word's pronunciation and part of speech. If the word has multiple meanings, they are also included. Note that some words may function as more than one part of speech, and that function may affect their meaning.

1. **campaign** (kam pān') *n:* **1.** a series of military operations. **2.** a series of activities for some specific purpose: *a political campaign. v:* **3.** to serve in or go on a campaign.

2. **capital** (kap' i til) *n:* **1.** the city or town that is the official seat of government of a country, state, etc. **2.** a city regarded as being of special importance in some field or activity: *the horse-racing capital.* **3.** CAPITAL LETTER. **4.** wealth, as in money or property. **5.** excellent or first-rate: *a capital hotel.*

3. **circumstance** (sûr' kəm stans') *n:* **1.** a condition or factor that accompanies, determines, or modifies a fact or event; an influencing factor. **2.** Usu. **circumstances:** financial status or means.

Janet Williams

4. **determine** (di tûr′ min) *v:* **1.** to settle or resolve, as an argument or question. **2.** to conclude after reasoning or observation. **3.** to decide upon.

5. **effective** (i fek′ tiv) *adj:* **1.** producing the desired result. **2.** being in force, as a law. **3.** producing a striking impression: *an effective use of color.*

6. **establish** (i stab′ lish) *v:* **1.** to bring into being; found; institute: *to establish a church.* **2.** to set oneself up, as in business. **3.** to show to be valid or true; prove: *to establish the facts.* **4.** to cause to be accepted or recognized: *to establish a tradition.* **5.** to bring about: *to establish order.*

7. **frequently** (frē′ kwənt lē) *adj:* often; many times; at short intervals.

8. **indicate** (in′ di kāt) *v:* **1.** to be a sign of. **2.** to point out or point to: *to indicate a place on a map.* **3.** to demonstrate the condition of: *The symptoms indicate the presence of disease.*

9. **requirement** (ri kwīr′ mənt) *n:* something needed or demanded.

10. **significant** (sig nif′ i kənt) *adj:* **1.** important; of consequence. **2.** having a meaning.

Exercise 4: Choose from Multiple Meanings

Some of the words you are studying in this chapter have several meanings. In this exercise, first determine which word best completes each sentence. (You will use words more than once.) Then indicate the number of the meaning from the word list that helped you make your choice.

a. campaign   b. capital   c. effective   d. establish

_b 1_ 1. The seniors enjoyed their class trip to visit the state
_____   _____.

_C 3_ 2. Academy award nominations are not always given to the
_____   most _____ films.

_D 3_ 3. The defense attorney tried to _____ an alibi
_____   for his client for the time of the murder.

_C 4_ 4. The dog trainer emphasized that reward and praise are
_____   very _____ methods of encouraging a dog's
         obedient behavior.

_B 4_ 5. Determining that the couple had insufficient
_____   _____ for the down payment on the house, the
         bank officer denied their mortgage application.

_D₁_   6. Rutgers University was one of the first colleges

_____ed in the United States.

_A₃_   7. After receiving encouragement from friends, family, and

supporters, Lamar Alexander decided to _____ for the presidency.

_C₂_   8. The registrar announced that the tuition increase would be

_____ at the beginning of the next semester.

_A₁_   9. The president presented the general with a medal in recognition of his fine leadership during the military

_____.

_D₄_ 10. The Latino custom of exchanging gifts on the Feast of the

Three Kings was _____ed long ago.

Exercise 5: Use the Word Correctly

The sentences below contain underlined words that you have studied. Indicate whether the words are used correctly (C) or incorrectly (I).

_I_   1. Once every decade, Ingrid makes one of her <u>frequent</u> visits to her sister's house.

_C_   2. As her <u>circumstances</u> changed, Francesca decided she could no longer contribute as much money to her church as she had in the past.

_I_   3. Once the therapist <u>established</u> the cause of Scott's distress, she was able to begin a course of treatment.

_I_   4. Teachers in the middle school decided to abandon their science program because it had been so <u>effective</u>.

_C_   5. A <u>significant</u> breakthrough in the fight against breast cancer is early detection.

_C_   6. Anna and Jorge enjoyed a <u>capital</u> meal at one of the city's excellent restaurants.

_I_   7. Since he did not meet the vision <u>requirement</u>, the Air Force recruiter told Gary he was eligible for pilot training.

8. Symptoms <u>indicate</u> that Dianne contracted a tropical viral disease when she visited Brazil.

 9. The advertising agency considered the <u>campaign</u> a success when sales tripled.

 10. The judge <u>determined</u> that the jury should hear the defendant's testimony in its entirety.

Exercise 6: Write Your Own Sentences

Write a sentence that uses each of the words you studied in this chapter in a way that indicates your understanding of the word's meaning.

1. A fact was <u>established</u> from the DNA of a serial killer

2. Requiring to do this English course is <u>significant</u> to my success

3. The presidential <u>campaign</u> among the Democrats was challenging

4. The <u>circumstances</u> that led to the evasion of Iraq has proven untrue.

5. Beheading people publicly was used as <u>capital</u> punishment during ancient days.

6. Flu <u>vaccination</u> given last year was effective

7. I would be able to meet all the <u>requirements</u> outlined for this semester.

8. ~~Frequently~~ speaking, I don't think I can continue doing this frequently.

9. My test result will <u>determine</u> whether I can make it or not.

10. His attitude <u>indicates</u> that he has no sense of humor

CHAPTER 2

This chapter continues your study of general, high-frequency words that you can expect to encounter in your academic and recreational reading. Most cannot easily be defined by a knowledge of word parts, nor are they tied to a particular field of study. Since you will meet these words in textual reading situations, they are first presented here in context. You will be asked first to write a definition of the word according to how it is used in the sentence and passage. Then you will complete a matching exercise that will help you confirm your conclusions about the word's meanings. You can then review the word list, which gives dictionary-type definitions. Finally, you will complete more practice exercises to help you learn the words.

Read the following passage through completely. Then return to the beginning and write your definition for each numbered and underlined word.

Tea and Conversation

During her first semester at college, Janice received an invitation to a (1) <u>traditional</u> tea held at the home of her English professor. She felt a bit nervous and wondered if she would fit in with the (2) <u>literary</u> types she expected to meet there. As she entered the front hallway, she was pleased that she (3) <u>recognized</u> two of her classmates, as well as several professors and local authors. Her (4) <u>expression</u> must have revealed her anxiety, as Professor Valley came over at once and steered her into a group of politically active professors and students. They were discussing human rights violations in countries to which the United States provides financial assistance. One particularly irate sociologist insisted that the United States should impose trade (5) <u>sanctions</u> against any country that does not demonstrate an immediate improvement in its human rights policies. Although several others in the group agreed, most felt that the countries ought to be given a chance to (6) <u>phase</u> out some of these unacceptable policies. A theology instructor with a strong interest in helping people in developing nations felt our role should be as instruments of divine (7) <u>providence</u> in helping to protect God's creatures. (8) <u>Nevertheless,</u> he, too, felt that cutting off funds immediately might harm the very people we are trying to help. For example, some of the funds support health programs and (9) <u>vocational</u> education. As Janice was drawn into the very stimulating discussion, she forgot about her (10) <u>initial</u> nervousness and enjoyed the lively exchange of opinions.

Exercise 1: Define

Write your definition for each word as it is used in the passage.

1. traditional   *inherited, belief & customs said by mouth w/out written instruction*
2. literary   *Be able to read & write / Laberature.*
3. recognized   *To notice, to identify*
4. expression   *Something that represents signs / thought*
5. sanctions   *penalties, to make you agree to to messes*
6. phase   *a stage, to schedule*
7. providence   *God's power on the universe,*

8. nevertheless *However,*

9. vocational *a training school in a specific career.*

10. initial *Beginning, first letter of names*

Exercise 2: Match

Match the terms in Column A with their definitions in Column B.

Column A	*Column B*
c 1. traditional	a. related to career training
d 2. initial	b. care; watchfulness
e 3. literary	c. formal; handed down by custom
j 4. recognize	d. first; at the beginning
i 5. expression	e. related to literature or writing
h 6. sanctions	f. a stage; to schedule
f 7. phase	g. however; in spite of
b 8. providence	h. penalties
g 9. nevertheless	i. facial appearance
a 10. vocational	j. to identify; to remember

Exercise 3: Fill In

Fill in the letter of the word that best completes each sentence.

a. expressions	d. nevertheless	g. recognize	i. traditional
b. initial	e. phase	h. sanctions	j. vocational
c. literary	f. providence		

_____ 1. Sean's parents hoped the period of rebellion he was going

through was just a ___*e*___ that would soon pass.

_____ 2. At first, Diego did not ___*g*___ his cousin since he hadn't
seen her for several years and she had changed considerably.

_____ 3. Samantha's guidance counselor advised her to attend

___*j*___ school since she had already decided on her
career.

_____ 4. Although Judy did not consider herself a ___*υ*___ person, she found that she enjoyed her English classes best.

_____ 5. ___*h*___ were imposed on members of the tribe who refused to adhere to local customs.

_____ 6. Lisa and Tony decided that their wedding ceremony and reception would be more ___*i*___ than modern.

_____ 7. Debbie insisted she had no desire to attend college; ___*d*___, her mother requested catalogs and applications for her.

_____ 8. José's ___*b*___ reaction to the proposal softened as he realized that several committee members were willing to help with the project.

_____ 9. After experiencing several personal tragedies, the Martin family decided to place their trust in divine ___*f*___.

_____ 10. Even though Mai Lin's command of English was quite good, she could still be confused by the use of certain ___*a*___.

WORD LIST

The following list gives dictionary-type definitions of the words you are studying in this chapter. Each entry includes the word's pronunciation and part of speech. If the word has multiple meanings, they are also included. Note that some words may function as more than one part of speech, and that function may affect their meaning.

1. **expression** (eks prĕ′ shən) *n:* **1.** the act of communicating ideas or feelings. **2.** a particular manner of speech. **3.** a sign or symbol. **4.** facial appearance that conveys feeling. **5.** a word or phrase.

2. **initial** (i nish′ əl) *adj:* **1.** occurring first. *n:* **2.** the first letter of a person's name, usu. *initials. v:* **3.** to sign one's initials, as to a document.

3. **literary** (lit′ ə rer ē) *adj:* **1.** related to literature or writing. **2.** well-read.

4. **nevertheless** (nev′ ər thə less′) *adv:* however; yet; in spite of.

5. **phase** (fāz) *n:* **1.** one of a sequence of aspects or changing conditions. **2.** a particular stage of development. **3.** one of the recurring visible forms of the moon or other planets.

6. **providence** (prov′ i dəns) *n:* **1.** the divine care God exercises over the universe. **2.** (*cap.*) God. **3.** foresight or careful management.

7. **recognize** (rek′ əg nīze) *v:* **1.** to acknowledge as someone or something previously known. **2.** to perceive on the basis of past experience. **3.** to give permission to speak. **4.** to acknowledge the independence or legitimacy of a nation. **5.** to offer appreciation, as in the form of a reward or tribute.

8. **sanction** (sank′ shən) *n:* **1.** authoritative approval or permission. **2.** a penalty intended to force compliance. **3.** *usu.* **sanctions** *plural* measures adopted to force a nation that is violating international law to stop.

9. **traditional** (trə dish′ ə nəl) *adj:* **1.** related to history or that which is handed down. **2.** referring to beliefs or practices that are customary or acceptable.

10. **vocational** (vō kā′ shən əl) *adj:* related to career or occupation, usu. in the form of instruction, training, or counseling.

Exercise 4: Choose from Multiple Meanings

Some of the words you are studying in this chapter have several meanings. In this exercise, first determine which word best completes each sentence. (You will use words more than once.) Then indicate the number of the meaning from the word list that helped you make your choice.

a. expression   b. initial   c. phase   d. recognize   e. sanction

_b₂_   1. At the real estate closing, Pat had to ___b___ each page of the document before she received her check for the sale of her house.
_____

_C₂_   2. At the height of her "terrible two" ___c___, Megan's favorite word was "No!"
_____

_a₄_   3. Andy could tell from his boss's ___a___ that he was in big trouble for arriving late for work.
_____

_d₃_   4. After the candidates' introductory speeches, members of

the audience were ___d___d so they could ask questions.
_____

_b₁_   5. Although Kesha's ___b___ impression of her Chemistry professor was not favorable, she grew to appreciate his knowledge and concern.
_____

_____ 6. The minister decided to donate a substantial portion of
_____   the church's funds to an emergency relief fund without

          the congregation's _____ *d* _____.

_____ 7. On his first trip down south, Darnel enjoyed the slower
_____   pace, warm weather, and the frequently heard

          _____ *a* _____, "Y'all come back soon."

_____ 8. The United States imposed _____ *e* _____s against
_____   Iran for its alleged promotion of terrorist activities.

_____ 9. At the reunion, members of the class wore buttons with their

_____   graduation pictures so they could _____ *d* _____ each
           other.

_____ 10. The director of the science museum organized a night sky

_____   watch tour during the moon's crescent _____ *c* _____.

Exercise 5: Use the Word Correctly

The sentences below contain underlined words that you have studied. Indicate whether the words are used correctly (C) or incorrectly (I).

_C_   1. Camellia resolved to seek <u>vocational</u> counseling in an effort
         to improve her relationship with her boyfriend.

_C_   2. Lucia and Dan revisited the tree where he had carved their
         <u>initials</u> in a heart when they were twelve years old.

_C_   3. <u>Expressions</u> of sympathy came in the form of cards, flowers,
         donations, and food, as neighbors tried to console the family
         after their child's death.

_I_   4. At the end of the semester, students were expected to complete a report summarizing their projects and describing
         their <u>providence</u>.

_I_   5. As a result of the family's <u>literary</u> interests, they subscribed
         to cable television and appreciated the fine sports coverage.

_C_   6. When young people enter their adolescent <u>phase</u>, they often
         experience emotional turmoil.

_____I_____ 7. Tim's parents told him that they could not <u>sanction</u> his decision to tour the country on a motorcycle instead of attending college.

_____C_____ 8. April was extremely nervous on opening night; <u>nevertheless</u>, the critics raved about her performance.

_____I_____ 9. Interested in studying the <u>traditional</u> ways of his people, Tayo purchased a book entitled *New Techniques in Weaving and Basketry*.

_____C_____ 10. <u>Recognized</u> as a noted scholar of the former Soviet Union, the retired professor was invited to address the international conference.

Exercise 6: Write Your Own Sentences

Write a sentence that uses each of the words you studied in this chapter in a way that indicates your understanding of the word's meaning.

1. The intial agreement b/w Joe & his parents was is to attend go College.

2. I could tell from the expressions from my teacher's face, that was happy leaving my assignment undone.

3. Due to literary teaching, my life has changed dramatically. was

4. Sanctions imposed on Libya due to bombing of the American airlines.

5. Being an African had made me to have too much beliefs traditional beliefs

6. By seeing president Bush on TV pequently had made me to recognized him in public.

7. Having gone to vocational training Caused me to become a successful mechanics.

8. After suffering from a broken leg, Nevertheless I still made Na soccer team.

9. I received note from a doctor, my intial beliefs was, I wouldn't be checked by any female Doctor.

10. His X-rays result indicates that everything was going as planned.

J. WILLIAMS

CHAPTER 3

Some of the words in this chapter contain word parts you may know. Since you are meeting the words in context, you have the opportunity to use both your knowledge of word parts and context clues to figure out their meanings. When you have several options as to which word attack strategy you will use, select the one that works best in the situation. Or, use both. Although you probably will not encounter as many as 10 unfamiliar words in a short passage, try to complete the first exercise as if you were actually reading the passage as an assignment or for information or pleasure. Then figure out the words' meanings as if you needed to do that to continue to read in a meaningful way.

Read the following passage through completely. Then return to the beginning and write your definition for each numbered and underlined word.

A New Business Venture

Rachel's lifetime dream was to own her own restaurant. After working in the business for six years as a waitress, chef, and restaurant manager, she felt (1) <u>capable</u> of venturing out on her own. A (2) <u>contemporary</u> of hers who had worked in several of the same places and had opened a cafe two years ago volunteered help and advice. Max said the first step in the (3) <u>procedure</u> would be to find a location. They began their search in a business district that might provide lunchtime customers. At first they looked at some (4) <u>commercial</u> space with a high rent and a (5) <u>substantial</u> monthly (6) <u>maintenance</u> fee. Both Max and Rachel felt it important to keep expenses low until they had an idea how much business she could generate. They turned their attention to a transitional neighborhood with a mixture of renovated buildings and "handyman specials." In addition, new arrivals to the neighborhood were young professionals who were opening small businesses and living nearby. A large empty lot was purchased by the Bank of (7) <u>Commerce</u> and Trade, and local government officials had approved their plans for a corporate headquarters building. With reasonable property prices and (8) <u>potential</u> for future growth, Rachel decided to buy a small luncheonette to develop into a casual neighborhood restaurant serving lunch and dinner. After making an offer on the property, she made an appointment with the loan officer at the local bank. Armed with her résumé, letters of recommendation, and a comprehensive business plan, a well- (9) <u>groomed</u> Rachel, dressed in her "make a good impression" suit, met with Mr. Wilson. In an (10) <u>apparent</u> vote of confidence, he approved her loan on the spot, and Rachel's restaurant was on its way.

Exercise 1: Define

Write your definition for each word as it is used in the passage.

1. capable   *able, qualified, prepare*
2. contemporary   *Some one in the same age, peers*
3. procedure   *a way of doing Something*
4. commercial   *related to business*

5. substantial   *ample, considerable*
6. maintenance   *up keep; support*
7. commerce   *trade, buying & selling good*
8. potential   *something that can develop*
9. groomed   *clean, neat; attractive)*
10. apparent   *Obvious, seen easily*

Exercise 2: Match

Match the terms in Column A with their definitions in Column B.

Column A	*Column B*
1. procedure *j*	a. trade; buying and selling goods
2. potential *d*	b. obvious, easily seen
3. capable *g*	c. one of the same time or age
4. substantial *f*	d. something that can develop
5. maintenance *e*	e. upkeep; support
6. contemporary *c*	f. ample; considerable
7. commercial *h*	g. competent; qualified
8. commerce *a*	h. related to business
9. apparent *b*	i. cleaned; neat, attractive
10. groomed *i*	j. a way of doing something; a series of steps

Exercise 3: Fill In

Fill in the letter of the word that best completes each sentence.

a. commercial   d. apparent   g. contemporary   i. capable
b. potential   e. procedure   h. substantial   j. groomed
c. maintenance   f. commerce

_____ b _____   1. Failing to live up to her _____, Karen's poor grades resulted in her dismissal from school.

_C_   2. Until they had lived through one winter in the old farm

house, Roy and Ellen had no idea of the ___C___ it
would require.

_h_   3. Inheriting a _____ sum of money from his grandfather
enabled Derek to attend medical school.

_g_   4. Paula preferred the art works of the great masters to the

more _____ paintings she saw at the Museum of
Modern Art.

_d_   5. In an _____ upset, the defending world champion was
easily defeated by a newcomer.

_i_   6. After completing a baby-sitting course offered by the local

YMCA, Jonathan felt completely _____ of watching
neighbors' children.

_f_   7. Maria knew that her fluency in Spanish would be an asset to

her future career in international _____.

_e_   8. Negligence in following the correct _____ resulted in
invalid test results and jeopardized the scientific study.

_a_   9. Dewey's lobster business profited more from his _____
sales to restaurants than from his retail sales to walk-in
customers.

_j_   10. At the training session for new managers, the instructors

stressed the need for well-_____ and courteous
employees.

WORD LIST

The following list gives dictionary-type definitions of the words you are
studying in this chapter. Each entry includes the word's pronunciation and
part of speech. If the word has multiple meanings, they are also included.
Note that some words may function as more than one part of speech, and
that function may affect their meaning.

1. **apparent** (ə par′ ənt) *adj:* easily seen; visible; obvious.

2. **capable** (kā′ pə bəl) *adj:* competent; qualified; having power to do
something.

3. **commerce** (kom′ ərs) *n:* the buying and selling of goods or commodities; trade.

4. **commercial** (kə mûr′ shəl) *adj:* **1.** related to commerce or trade. **2.** designed for profit. *n:* **3.** a radio or television advertisement.

5. **contemporary** (kən tem′ pə rer ē) *adj:* **1.** occurring at the same time. **2.** belonging to the same period. **3.** current; modern. *n:* **4.** a person of the same time or age. **5.** a person of the modern age.

6. **groom** (gro̅o̅m) *v:* **1.** to clean and care for. **2.** to make one's appearance neat. **3.** to train or prepare for a particular role. *n:* **4.** a person employed to take care of horses. **5.** a bridegroom; a man newly married or about to be married.

7. **maintenance** (mān′ tə nəns) *n:* **1.** the act of keeping in good repair. **2.** means of support. **3.** the work of keeping roads, machinery, etc. in good condition.

8. **potential** (pə ten′ shəl) *adj:* **1.** possible but not yet realized. *n:* **2.** a possible development.

9. **procedure** (prə sē′ jər) *n:* 1. a manner of doing something. **2.** a series of steps. **3.** an established way of doing business.

10. **substantial** (sub stan′ shəl) *adj:* **1.** solid; real. **2.** valuable. **3.** ample; considerable.

Exercise 4: Choose from Multiple Meanings

Several of the words you are studying in this chapter have a variety of meanings. In this exercise, first determine which word best completes each sentence. (You will use words more than once.) Then indicate the number of the meaning from the word list that helped you make your choice.

a. commercial   c. groom   e. maintenance
b. contemporary   d. potential

_e2_ 1. After her divorce, Pat received a monthly _e_____
       check from her ex-husband.

_a 3_ 2. At the most critical point in the hockey game, a
       _____ _a_____ interrupted the play.

_4_ 3. When the owner of the riding stable decided to expand,
       she hired an additional _b c_____ to help with
       the horses.

_2_   4. Few people realized its _____d_____ for growth when the first of the Wal-Mart stores opened.

_3_   5. After graduating from high school, Steve accepted a job with the school board as a _____e_____ worker and cared for the buildings where he had studied.

_4_   6. The work of Mary Cassatt, a _____b_____ of the great Impressionist painters, is beginning to receive the attention it deserves.

_2_   7. As a _____a_____ artist, Jim produced illustrations for the weekly sales brochures.

_3_   8. At the beginning of the summer, the camp director told Wendy she planned to _____c_____ her for the job of arts and crafts supervisor for the following year.

_1_   9. Quick thinking averted a _____d_____ disaster as Abdul threw a blanket over the burning curtains and put out the fire.

_____ 10. Although she had thoroughly enjoyed the poetry she read in school, Laura found herself confused as she listened to the
_3_   _____b_____ poet read his work.

Exercise 5: Use the Word Correctly

The sentences below contain underlined words that you have studied. Indicate whether the words are used correctly (C) or incorrectly (I).

_c_   1. Though nervous about learning to sail, Emily's <u>capable</u> instructor gently reassured her.

_c_   2. Since Marta did not follow the correct registration <u>procedure</u>, her name did not appear on her professors' class rosters.

_I_   3. Planning for a career in <u>commerce</u>, Vadid applied to schools that specialized in marine biology.

_I_   4. Greg received a <u>substantial</u> tax refund and deposited the check for $5.75 in his checking account.

_C_   5. When Connie bought her first sheepdog, she learned how to <u>groom</u> him so that his coat did not become tangled and matted.

_I_   6. Silas often visited the cemetery and placed flowers on the graves of his <u>contemporaries</u> who had died over a hundred years ago.

_C_   7. <u>Apparently</u>, Paul was pleased to see his parents as he jumped out of the car and threw his arms around them.

_C_   8. The purchase price of the snowplow included a <u>maintenance</u> contract that covered all servicing and repairs for the first year.

_I_   9. The owner of the building advertised <u>commercial</u> space for rent with two bedrooms, a terrace, and a fully equipped kitchen.

_C_   10. Tina's first gymnastic coach thought she showed great <u>potential</u>, even at the age of five.

Exercise 6: Write Your Own Sentences

Write a sentence that uses each of the words you studied in this chapter in a way that indicates your understanding of the word's meaning.

1. _____

2. _____

3. _____

4. _____

5. _____

6. _____

7. _____

8. _____

9. _____

10. _____

CHAPTER 4

The general words in this chapter and in the other chapters in this section can be called high-frequency words. That means that they occur more often than other words in written English. Many high-frequency words have multiple meanings. For example, in this chapter, you will study the word components. Although any definition of the word includes the notion of parts, it can be used in very different contexts. It may refer to word parts, parts of a stereo system, or the ingredients in a recipe. As a result, you may come across this word in a variety of different types of writing. Of course, the words with the highest frequencies, like a, the, is, he, etc., are so common that everyone knows and uses them. They have not been included. It would be foolish to study the meanings of words you already know when there are so many other interesting and useful words you could be learning.

Chapter 4 & 6 TEST on Tuesday

Read the following passage through completely. Then return to the beginning and write your definition for each numbered and underlined word.

Social Programs in the United States

People who have grown up in the United States often have very strong opinions about government social programs. Their (1) <u>interpretation</u> of the value of such programs often corresponds to the (2) <u>generation</u> they belong to. For example, individuals approaching retirement usually feel (3) <u>entitled</u> to Social Security checks since they have been paying into the system for many years. A group of senior citizens will also show great emotional (4) <u>intensity</u> about proposed cuts in their Medicare health benefits. On the other hand, young mothers may believe a Head Start program for their children is more (5) <u>vital</u> than the programs that serve the elderly. Yet another opinion may be held by a young professional who sees his (6) <u>wage</u> earnings decreased by taxes to provide for the (7) <u>welfare</u> of others. One disgruntled accountant analyzed the (8) <u>conventional</u> pay stubs and income tax returns of 10 of his clients. When he divided the deductions into (9) <u>components</u> that benefited the wage-earner directly and those that primarily benefited others, his findings confirmed what he believed. For this particular group of employees, for every (10) <u>minute</u> the worker earned money for himself, he worked several minutes for the benefit of others. Those who preach the doctrine of social responsibility hold that every member of a society benefits from programs that improve the quality of life for its less fortunate members.

Exercise 1: Define

Write your definition for each word as it is used in the passage.

1. interpretation *one point of view or analysis*
2. generation *group of people in the same age group.*
3. entitled *having a right to something*
4. intensity *Concentration, or force*
5. vital *very important*
6. wage *salary, earning*
7. welfare *a social program that takes care of the poor people*
8. conventional *acceptible, traditional*

9. components *parts*

10. minute *60 seconds*

Exercise 2: Match

Match the terms in Column A with their definitions in Column B.

Column A	Column B
1. entitled *f*	a. view; outlook
2. intensity *h*	b. period of 60 seconds
3. vital *e*	c. parts
4. wage *g*	d. established; approved
5. components *c*	e. essential; important
6. interpretation *a*	f. deserving by right
7. generation *i*	g. earnings
8. minute *b*	h. strength or power, especially of feeling
9. welfare *j*	i. a group of individuals born at about the same time
10. conventional *d*	j. aid, as in money, clothing, etc., to those in need

Exercise 3: Fill In

Fill in the letter of the word that best completes each sentence.

a. components   d. generation   g. wage   i. vital
b. conventional   e. interpretation   h. welfare   j. minute
c. entitled   f. intensity

_*i*_   1. The emergency medical technician checked for the accident

victim's _____ signs as soon as he was removed from the car.

_*d*_   2. Henri's great-grandmother was the only representative of

her _____ at the family reunion.

g   3. Economists use the _____ and price index as one of their measures when they analyze the health of the economy.

e   4. Elaine's _____ of her new neighbor's behavior was that she was unfriendly, but Bill thought she was probably shy.

f   5. Not one _____ longer could Jamie gaze at the chocolate cream pie without cutting into it.

c   6. Even after he left home, found a job, and rented an apartment, Omar felt _____ to have his mother do his laundry.

a   7. The salesclerk in the music store urged Chuck to try out various _____ until he assembled the stereo system with the best sound.

b   8. Sonya's wedding took place in a field with barefoot guests, but her sister Ann's marriage ceremony was more _____.

h   9. The angry politician charged that the _____ program had made people lazy and was responsible for most of the country's ills.

f   10. Alicia delivered her lines in the play with such _____ that she felt exhausted after every performance.

WORD LIST

The following list gives dictionary-type definitions of the words you are studying in this chapter. Each entry includes the word's pronunciation and part of speech. If the word has multiple meanings, they are also included. Note that some words may function as more than one part of speech, and that function may affect their meaning.

1. **component** (kəm pō′ nənt) *n:* **1.** part; ingredient; constituent. *adj:* **2.** serving as a part of something.

2. **conventional** (kən ven′ shən əl) *adj:* **1.** generally approved by custom. **2.** established as acceptable.

3. **entitled** (en tīt′ ld) *adj:* having a right to something.

4. **generation** (jen ə rā′ shən) *n:* **1.** the act of bringing into existence. **2.** offspring having the same parents and constituting a stage of descent. **3.** a group

of contemporaries. **4.** the average time interval between the birth of parents and their children.

5. **intensity** (in ten′ sət ē) *n:* **1.** great concentration, force, or power. **2.** the measure of energy or force.

6. **interpretation** (in tər prə tā′ shən) *n:* **1.** the process of giving meaning to something; an explanation **2.** an individual representation, as in a work of art or performance.

7. **minute** (min′ ət) *n:* **1.** a unit of time equal to 60 seconds. **2.** any very short period of time. **3.** a specific instant of time.
(mī′ nōōt′) *adj:* **4.** exceedingly small. **5.** not important.

8. **vital** (vī′ təl) *adj:* **1.** necessary; essential. **2.** necessary for the continuation of life. **3.** lively.

9. **wage** (wāj) *n:* **1.** payment for work done, usu. pl. *v:* **2.** to carry on, as to wage war.

10. **welfare** (wel′ fâr) *n:* 1. general well-being. **2.** public assistance in the form of clothing, money, etc.

Exercise 4: Choose from Multiple Meanings

Some of the words you are studying in this chapter have several meanings. In this exercise, first determine which word best completes each sentence. (You will use words more than once.) Then indicate the number of the meaning from the word list that helped you make your choice.

   a. generation   b. interpretation   c. minute   d. welfare   e. intensity

_____   1. During the custody hearing, the judge indicated that her

_____   decision would be based on the ____*b*____ of the children.

_____   2. The ____*e*____ of the approaching car's headlights blinded Josh and caused him to swerve off the road.

_____

_____   3. Mr. Schneider, the science teacher, was delighted with the purchase of 10 new microscopes that allowed his students

_____   to observe ____*a*____ particles.

_____   4. Although there were several witnesses to the plane crash,

_____   each one's ____*b*____ differed from the others'.

_____ 5. After losing her job as a waitress, Barbara received

_____   _____d_____ checks for two months until she
could find another job.

_____ 6. Don believed a _____ gap contributed to the
difficulty he had communicating with his son.

_____

_____ 7. Chita Rivera's _____ of the title role in _The
Kiss of the Spider Woman_ differed from her successor's.

_____

_____ 8. The soccer team played with such _____ that
the players seemed oblivious of the pouring rain.

_____

_____ 9. Each _____ of the underwater dive cost $1,000
to pay for the divers, cameras, and metal detectors used in
_____   the search for treasure.

_____ 10. At one time, many people believed that _____
of electricity through nuclear power would be cost effective.

_____

Exercise 5: Use the Word Correctly

The sentences below contain underlined words that you have studied. Indicate whether the words are used correctly (C) or incorrectly (I).

_____ 1. As an American citizen, Carl thought he was <u>entitled</u> to preference over foreign students applying to the state university.

_____ 2. During the chess match, the <u>intensity</u> of Bobby's eyes reflected his casual attitude toward this match.

_____ 3. The king decided to <u>wage</u> war against his northern neighbor in spite of the lives that would be lost.

_____ 4. Health insurance is an important <u>component</u> of the company's benefit package that it uses to attract capable employees.

_____ 5. Candidates for the astronaut training program filled out applications that included their <u>vital</u> statistics such as height, weight, age, and vision.

_____ 6. The <u>conventional</u> minister earned a reputation as one who tried experimental music and audience participation at his services.

_____ 7. Concerned for the <u>welfare</u> of his opponent, the prizefighter agreed to delay the match so he could receive a medical evaluation.

_____ 8. After a thorough <u>interpretation</u>, the detective turned over all of his findings to the district attorney.

_____ 9. Carol's high school classmates who lived on the other side of town belonged to a different <u>generation</u>.

_____ 10. Each <u>minute</u> that the recycling plant stays idle costs the company money.

Exercise 6: Write Your Own Sentences

Write a sentence that uses each of the words you studied in this chapter in a way that indicates your understanding of the word's meaning.

1. _____

2. _____

3. _____

4. _____

5. _____

6. _____

7. _____

8. _____

9. _____

10. _____

CHAPTER 5

As you continue your study of high-frequency words, you may come across words that are synonyms for more common words. For example, in this chapter you will study the words *expenditures* and *precision*. You probably know and use their synonyms: *expenses* and *exactness* or *clarity*. Some students question the need to learn more words that mean the same thing. There are two reasons. The first is that, as a listener and reader, the choice of words used is not yours. For effective communication, you need to know the meanings of many words you may read or hear even though you may not choose to use them yourself. The second reason has to do with the nature of the English language. There are many synonyms in English, but each usually has a particular emphasis or interpretation that makes it appropriate to use in specific situations. Writers and speakers of English have the advantage of choosing from an array of words so that they can better convey their exact meaning. As a writer and speaker, if you have more words in your vocabulary, you will be able to say and write exactly what you mean. You will also be able to introduce some variety into your speech and written work.

Read the following passage through completely. Then return to the beginning and write your definition for each numbered and underlined word.

Discrimination at the Fitness Center

Last September, a lawsuit was filed demanding that a local health and fitness club establish an (1) integration plan. The plaintiffs claimed that women and male minority group members who applied for admission received either little (2) recognition or a (3) mere rejection slip. After the judge heard (4) testimony from several witnesses, she invited the attorneys from both sides into her (5) chamber for a private conversation. She explained that the claims of discrimination had to be supported with (6) precision. For example, a black man who was not accepted as a member would have to show that a white man with the same or lesser qualifications was admitted. She indicated that the (7) burden of proof lay with the plaintiffs. The attorneys who represented the plaintiffs felt they would have no trouble producing evidence of a pattern of discrimination and demanded access to the club's files to support their case. When the attorneys for the club owners told their clients that the (8) expenditures needed to defend the case could run quite high, they decided to settle. Part of the agreement included a (9) provision that the club set up a recruitment program to attract women and minorities. When the plaintiffs were awarded free memberships in the club, they felt that their mission had been (10) accomplished.

Exercise 1: Define

Write your definition for each word as it is used in the passage.

1. integration   _the act of bringing together_
2. recognition   _acknowledgement_
3. mere   _bring nothing more or less than, a rifle_
4. testimony   _evidence, a declaration_
5. chamber   _enclosed space or consultation room_
6. precision   _exactness_
7. burden   _load, responsibility_
8. expenditures   _what is paid out_

9. provision   *a measure taken beforehand /stipulation*
10. accomplished   *achieved*

Exercise 2: Match

Match the terms in Column A with their definitions in Column B.

Column A	Column B
1. integration *d*	a. exactness
2. mere *f*	b. what is paid out
3. provision *h*	c. load; responsibility
4. testimony *j*	d. the act of bringing together
5. chamber *i*	e. achieved
6. precision *a*	f. being nothing more or less than; a trifle
7. expenditures *b*	g. acknowledgment
8. accomplished *e*	h. a measure taken beforehand or stipulated
9. burden *c*	i. an enclosed space or consultation room
10. recognition *g*	j. evidence; a declaration

Exercise 3: Fill In

Fill in the letter of the word that best completes each sentence.

a. precision   d. testimony   g. chamber   i. integration
b. provision   e. recognition   h. mere   j. expenditures
c. burden   f. accomplished

___*c*___ 1. After her mother's death, the _____ of caring for her younger sister fell to Margaret.

___*j*___ 2. When the restaurant owners realized that the _____ had been greater than the profits for three years in a row, they closed their doors.

___b___ 3. In his will, Dr. Morse included a _____ that all of his books be given to the town library.

___i___ 4. Establishing magnet schools was one of the methods the school system used to achieve racial _____.

___d___ 5. The eyewitness's convincing _____ led to a murder conviction.

___f___ 6. Kay decided she would retire after she had _____ her goal of accumulating $2 million.

___e___ 7. In _____ for the many hours of help and advice she had provided, the newspaper staff presented the adviser with an engraved silver bowl.

___g___ 8. Everyone in the courtroom stood up as the judge entered from his _____.

___h___ 9. The salesman said, "For a _____ $425 per month, you can be the proud owner of this beautiful car."

___a___ 10. Photographs taken by a camera in the satellite enabled scientists to observe and chart features of the moon with greater _____ than ever before.

WORD LIST

The following list gives dictionary-type definitions of the words you are studying in this chapter. Each entry includes the word's pronunciation and part of speech. If the word has multiple meanings, they are also included. Note that some words may function as more than one part of speech, and that function may affect their meaning.

1. **accomplish** (ə kom′ plish) *v:* to achieve; to bring to completion.

2. **burden** (bûr′ den) *n:* **1.** something that is carried; load. **2.** care; responsibility. *v:* **3.** to weigh down; to overload; to oppress.

3. **chamber** (chām′ bər) *n:* **1.** a room, esp. a bedroom. **2.** a judge's office. **3.** a hall used for meetings. **4.** an enclosed space or cavity. **5.** the part of a gun that holds the cartridge.

4. **expenditure** (ek spen′ də chər) *n:* **1.** the act or process of paying out or using up. **2.** the amount expended or paid.

5. **integration** (in tə grā′ shən) *n:* **1.** the process of bringing together or unifying. **2.** the act of opening up to all ethnic groups by ending segregation.

6. **mere** (mēr) *adj:* **1.** being nothing more or less than what is specified; **2.** a trifle.

7. **precision** (pri sizh′ ən) *n:* **1.** the quality or state of being exact; accuracy. *adj:* **2.** intended for use in precise measurement, as a *precision instrument* or *precision tool.*

8. **provision** (prə vizh′ ən) *n:* **1.** the act of providing. **2.** a measure taken beforehand. **3. provisions:** a supply of necessities, usu. food. **4.** a stipulation or qualification referring to something specific in an agreement. *v:* **5.** to supply with provisions.

9. **recognition** (rek əg nish′ ən) *n.:* **1.** the act of identifying someone or something as having been previously known. **2.** acknowledgment; special notice or attention.

10. **testimony** (tes′ tə mō nē) *n:* **1.** a declaration or affirmation of a fact. **2.** supporting evidence or proof. **3.** a declaration made by a witness under oath, esp. in court. **4.** a public declaration of a religious experience.

Exercise 4: Choose from Multiple Meanings

Some of the words you are studying in this chapter have several meanings. In this exercise, first determine which word best completes each sentence. (You will use words more than once.) Then indicate the number of the meaning from the word list that helped you make your choice.

a. provision   b. recognition   c. testimony   d. chamber   e. precision

_____ 1. For two hours after regaining consciousness, Kristina

_____ displayed no _____ of the people around her or her surroundings.

_____ 2. The race car driver insisted that all work on his car be

_____ performed by the same mechanic with _____ tools.

_____ 3. One _____ of the four-year scholarship was that the student must maintain a 3.0 academic average.

_____

_____ 4. In a hearing to determine whether to remove life-sustaining

_____ equipment, Georgia's husband's _____ about her wishes was very convincing.

_____ 5. After checking into the New England bed and breakfast inn,

the owner showed Reid his small _____ and
the bathroom down the hall.

_____ 6. At the religious revival meeting, many people came forward

_____ to offer _____ about how they had been saved.

_____ 7. In _____ of her generous contributions over
the years, the new wing of the hospital was named in honor
_____ of Greta Buchanan.

_____ 8. As a specialist in eye surgery, Dr. Martinez performs opera-

_____ tions that require the greatest _____.

_____ 9. Before setting out on the Appalachian Trail, the novice hiker
asked his more experienced companion to help him

_____ _____ his backpack.

_____ 10. Before the jury entered the courtroom, the judge held a

_____ meeting in her _____ with the attorneys.

Exercise 5: Use the Word Correctly

The sentences below contain underlined words that you have studied. Indicate whether the words are used correctly (C) or incorrectly (I).

_____ 1. Charlene told the judge that she could not properly care
for her three children with a <u>mere</u> $350 per month payment
from her ex-husband.

_____ 2. As a <u>precision</u> in her property deed, Lila was not allowed
to build a structure that would block her neighbor's water
view.

_____ 3. Unable to <u>accomplish</u> what he hoped for, Martin resigned
as president of the tenants' association.

_____ 4. As a result of the <u>integration</u> order, the college was able
to continue to prevent students from specific racial groups
from enrolling.

_____ 5. Including her salary as a waitress, her overtime pay,
and tips, Marcia's monthly <u>expenditure</u> totaled $1,550.

_____ 6. Dave and his sisters agreed to share the <u>burden</u> of caring for their seriously ill parents.

_____ 7. As a newly elected senator, Olympia entered the legislative <u>chamber</u> with a sense of awe.

_____ 8. A lack of <u>recognition</u> prevented Walter from learning how to operate the machinery and thereby losing his job.

_____ 9. Although he died at a young age, Carlton's <u>provision</u> for his children insured that they would be financially comfortable until adulthood.

_____ 10. Conflicting <u>testimony</u> about whether the policeman's attack of the robbery suspect was provoked or not confused the members of the jury.

Exercise 6: Write Your Own Sentences

Write a sentence that uses each of the words you studied in this chapter in a way that indicates your understanding of the word's meaning.

1. _____

2. _____

3. _____

4. _____

5. _____

6. _____

7. _____

8. _____

9. _____

10. _____

CHAPTER 6

The words in this chapter are truly college-level words. They are sufficiently specific to convey a particular meaning and thereby can help the writer or speaker convey his or her message effectively. Although you may not hear these words in casual conversations with your friends, they would surely be found in a dialogue between educated persons. You will come across them in the newspaper and hear them on serious radio broadcasts. In fact, you may find them useful in your own speaking and writing.

Read the following passage through completely. Then return to the beginning and write your definition for each numbered and underlined word.

Police Corruption Scandal

Last month, the mayor hired Police Commissioner Foley. He hoped a new leader with a mark of (1) <u>distinction</u> for his work in other cities would be able to handle the department's corruption scandal. Mayor Walker had intentionally chosen an (2) <u>external</u> candidate who would have no past connections to police officers or (3) <u>bureau</u> chiefs. Attempts to keep the scandal quiet failed when the city's biggest newspaper ran an (4) <u>editorial</u> condemning the widespread abuse of power by police officers. One example they included described how members of the (5) <u>vice</u> squad had confiscated a large amount of cocaine in a drug bust. Rather than turning over all the drugs as evidence, the officers kept half of the quantity and sold it for a sum in (6) <u>excess</u> of $250,000. Other specific charges (7) <u>varied</u> from the least serious, such as accepting free subway rides, to the disturbingly close relationship between some police officers and members of the mob. Commissioner Foley told the press he would make no (8) <u>assumptions</u> about anyone's guilt or innocence until a thorough investigation had been conducted. He explained that a problem of such magnitude warranted an (9) <u>investment</u> of time and energy that would assure the correct (10) <u>identification</u> of the guilty parties. He assured the mayor and the public that appropriate measures would be taken to punish those responsible, to remove criminals from the department, and to provide the city with the police protection it deserves.

Exercise 1: Define

Write your definition for each word as it is used in the passage.

1. distinction   *honor, of excellent*
2. external   *outside*
3. bureau   *department*
4. editorial   *news paper article w/ an opinion*
5. vice   *bad habit / illegal acts*
6. excess   *more than*

7. varied   _ranged, changed_

8. assumption _something believe before it is proved_

9. investment _money / something committed for future gain_

10. identification _art of pointing out to recognize someone_

Exercise 2: Match

Match the terms in Column A with their definitions in Column B.

Column A	Column B
_e_ 1. bureau	a. beyond the usual; more than
_g_ 2. external	b. a bad habit; immorality
_f_ 3. identification	c. an opinionated newspaper article
_j_ 4. investment	d. something taken for granted
_c_ 5. editorial	e. a government department
_a_ 6. excess	f. the act of being recognized
_i_ 7. varied	g. outside
_d_ 8. assumption	h. a characteristic difference
_h_ 9. distinction	i. changed; differed
_b_ 10. vice	j. that which is committed or used

Exercise 3: Fill In

Fill in the letter of the word that best completes each sentence.

a. editorial	d. vice	g. identification	i. excess
b. external	e. assumption	h. bureau	j. varied
c. distinction	f. investment		

_e_   1. The physics professor began her first lecture of the semester under the false _____ that all of her students had taken calculus.

_c_   2. The most important _____ between members and non-members of the club was the right to vote on policy issues.

_g_ 3. After the victim made a positive _____ of the robbery suspect, he was charged with the crime.

_d_ 4. Convinced that smoking was a _____ she should abandon, Rita visited an acupuncturist who tried to help her quit.

_j_ 5. The restaurant offered such a _____ menu that diners often had difficulty choosing.

_b_ 6. Before closing the deal, the prospective buyer of the paper company hired an accounting firm to do an _____ audit of its financial records.

_h_ 7. Faith feared she would face a long wait as she tried to renew her expired driver's license at the _____ of motor vehicles.

_a_ 8. The presidential candidate was delighted to read the _____ that endorsed her.

_i_ 9. _____ water caused by 12 days of heavy rain posed a serious threat to the wheat crop.

_f_ 10. Shortly after Steven was born, his parents began an _____ account to save money for his college education.

WORD LIST

The following list gives dictionary-type definitions of the words you are studying in this chapter. Each entry includes the word's pronunciation and part of speech. If the word has multiple meanings, they are also included. Note that some words may function as more than one part of speech, and that function may affect their meaning.

1. **assumption** (ə sum′ shən) *n.:* a statement accepted as true without proof.

2. **bureau** (byoor′ ō) *n.:* **1.** a chest of drawers. **2.** a government agency or department. **3.** an office that performs a specific duty.

3. **distinction** (dis tink′ shən) *n.:* **1.** the act of noting a difference; discrimination. **2.** a difference. **3.** a distinguishing factor or characteristic. **4.** personal excellence. **5.** honor.

4. **editorial** (ed i tôr′ ē əl) *n.:* an article in a newspaper expressing the opinion of the editor.

5. **excess** (ek′ ses) *n:* **1.** an amount beyond what is required; a surplus. **2.** overindulgence; intemperance.

6. **external** (eks tər′ nəl) *adj:* **1.** of or on the outside. **2.** pertaining to the outer self; superficial. **3.** arising from without; foreign.

7. **identification** (ī den′ tə fik ā shən) *n:* **1.** the act or process of being recognized. **2.** documentary proof of one's identity.

8. **investment** (in vest′ mənt) *n:* **1.** a commitment of money, time, or energy for future profit or gain. **2.** the money or property purchased.

9. **varied** (vâr′ ēd) *adj:* **1.** having variety or many types or forms; diverse. *v:* (past tense) **2.** changed; modified; altered.

10. **vice** (vīs) *n:* **1.** an immoral habit or trait. **2.** corruption, evil. **3.** one substituting for or replacing another, as a *vice-chairman*.

Exercise 4: Choose from Multiple Meanings

Some of the words you are studying in this chapter have several meanings. In this exercise, first determine which word best completes each sentence. (You will use words more than once.) Then indicate the number of the meaning from the word list that helped you make your choice.

a. identification   b. varied   c. vice   d. bureau   e. distinction

_____d_____ 1. The set of bedroom furniture included a double bed, two
_____ night stands, and a large _____.

_____b_____ 2. Marcel's mood _____ so much from day to
day that his co-workers never knew what to expect of him.

_____c_____ 3. Jane quickly realized that her role as _____
president of the association brought her more responsibilities than the president had.

_____e_____ 4. The professor tried to make a clear _____
between passing the final exam and passing the course.

_____a_____ 5. The clerk at the box office required Tom to show his
_____ before she would release the baseball tickets he had charged by telephone.

_____c_____ 6. Beth read that drug abuse is a _____ that
seems to run in families.

_e_   7. At the graduation ceremony, the president of the college announced that five students would graduate with

_____ _____ as a result of 4.0 averages.

_d_   8. Charlie contacted the _____ of records to obtain a copy of his birth certificate so he could apply for

_____ a passport.

_b_   9. To attract a large audience, the band director planned a

_____ _____ program of music to suit all tastes.

_e_   10. As part of her ornamental horticulture program, Marissa

_____ took a class on the _____ of wild plants and flowers.

Exercise 5: Use the Word Correctly

The sentences below contain underlined words that you have studied. Indicate whether the words are used correctly (C) or incorrectly (I).

_I_   1. The new department manager circulated an <u>external</u> memo among the members of her department asking for their cooperation.

_C_   2. The debris and rubble that fell on the earthquake victims made <u>identification</u> of the bodies almost impossible.

_I_   3. Keith's guitar lessons <u>varied</u> so that each week he practiced the same chords and songs over again.

^   _I_   4. The <u>editorial</u> about funding a new high school building presented the facts and allowed the readers to draw their own conclusions.

x   _I_   5. Felicia's mother's <u>assumption</u> that she had spent the night at a friend's house was proven false when she received a call from the police department.

_C_   6. The governor promised that she would tolerate no corruption or <u>vice</u> in her administration and appointments would be made on merit.

x   _C_   7. In the 1970s, an <u>excess</u> of gasoline caused drivers to line up at gas stations hours before they opened so they could purchase a few gallons.

X ___I___ 8. No <u>distinction</u> could be drawn between the students who had entered the school in kindergarten and those who transferred in later.

___C___ 9. One of the responsibilities of the <u>Bureau</u> of Indian Affairs is to provide educational opportunities.

___C___ 10. Because of unwise <u>investments</u>, Luke found that he could not afford to retire at the age of sixty-five and still keep up his mortgage payments.

Exercise 6: Write Your Own Sentences

Write a sentence that uses each of the words you studied in this chapter in a way that indicates your understanding of the word's meaning.

1. _____

2. _____

3. _____

4. _____

5. _____

6. _____

7. _____

8. _____

9. _____

10. _____

CHAPTER 7

The words you have been studying are high-frequency words found in written English. If you say that you don't often hear these words, your instincts are correct. There are interesting contrasts between written and spoken language. According to a study conducted by Hartvig Dahl, a mere 848 words account for 90 percent of spoken usage. In contrast, it takes nearly 8,000 words to account for 90 percent of written word use. We tend to use more conjunctions in speaking; that is, we string thoughts together with *ands, buts,* and *ors.* We don't use the articles *the* and *a* as often, but we use the pronoun *I* ten times as often as in writing. Not surprisingly, there is also a much higher incidence of profanity in spoken language than in written language.

Although you won't come close to learning the 8,000 most common words in written English, you can be assured that when you read, you will meet the words you have been studying.

Read the following passage through completely. Then return to the beginning and write your definition for each numbered and underlined word.

Is It in the Genes?

A university psychology professor has been studying the relative influences of heredity and environment on individuals. For the last 10 years, she has devoted (1) <u>virtually</u> all of her time to this project. She obtained some data about identical twins that had been separated at birth. Then she conducted her own study using a (2) <u>random</u> sample of siblings, one adopted and one biological child. She obtained (3) <u>parallel</u> data on these individuals to try to determine whether the genetic influence or a person's home environment plays a more (4) <u>prominent</u> role in shaping his or her development. (5) <u>Presumably</u>, the home environment that the biological child shared with his or her adopted sibling was the same. The separated twins, on the other hand, had the same genes but different home environments. The professor tried to estimate the (6) <u>probability</u> that, as adults, these twins and siblings would have similar talents, careers, and personality traits. She was amazed to see that the similarities in the separated twins' lives were much higher than her estimates predicted. Common marriage and divorce patterns, the number of children, career choices, and even similar senses of humor were found. In fact, in one case, a man was going through a divorce while his twin brother was (7) <u>simultaneously</u> going through the same experience, though they were not in contact with each other. When no such similar patterns were found for the nonbiological siblings, the professor concluded that most of these traits and tendencies were (8) <u>derived</u> from the individuals' genetic make-up. (9) <u>Inevitably</u>, the funding for the study ended before the professor would have liked. She is hoping to obtain grant money so that she can plan an (10) <u>extension</u> of the study that would allow her to follow the lives of these individuals over time.

Exercise 1: Define

Write your definition for each word as it is used in the passage.

1. virtually   *effectively*

2. random   *w/ no specific order*

3. parallel   *as a~~ fore reasonable assumptions~~*
                    two opposite thing that have similarity

4. prominent   *noticeable, standing out,*

5. presumably   *reasonable assumption*

6. probability   *likelihood*

7. simultaneously   *at the same time*

8. derived   *originated, came from*

9. inevitably   *inevitably bound to happen*

10. extension   *to prolong / act of making longer*

Exercise 2: Match

Match the terms in Column A with their definitions in Column B.

Column A	*Column B*
1. virtually	a. with no specific order 8
2. parallel	b. originated; came from 5
3. presumably	c. at the same time 9
4. prominent	d. noticeable; standing out 4
5. derived	e. likelihood 6
6. probability	f. bound to happen 7
7. inevitably	g. the act of making longer 10
8. random	h. as a reasonable assumption 3
9. simultaneously	i. in effect 1
10. extension	j. having a close resemblance 2

Exercise 3: Fill In

Fill in the letter of the word that best completes each sentence.

a. probability   d. virtually   g. extension   i. random
b. inevitably   e. parallel   h. prominent   j. presumably
c. derived   f. simultaneously

_i_   1. Winners of the door prize were chosen at _____ from
       ticket stubs that had been deposited in a basket by the
       entrance.

2. Marielena's friend marveled at her ability to juggle the demands of a full-time career and motherhood _____.

_c_ 3. After Webster had studied Latin for a semester, he realized how many English words are _____ from Latin.

_g_ 4. Larry received an _____ for filing his tax return while he was out of the country.

_d_ 5. _____ the whole town attended the beloved mayor's funeral.

_h_ 6. Pete chose to fly to Houston where his operation would be performed by one of the nation's most _____ surgeons.

_a_ 7. The _____ of a chance meeting with his cousin in Grand Central Station was slim, yet it happened to Ted.

_e_ 8. The two candidates for the position of president of the company had _____ careers in sales and management.

_j_ 9. Slippery roads _____ caused the accident, but since no one survived, we can't be sure.

_b_ 10. As her grandchildren started to leave, Ruth _____ detained them by asking what they would like for Christmas.

WORD LIST

The following list gives dictionary-type definitions of the words you are studying in this chapter. Each entry includes the word's pronunciation and part of speech. If the word has multiple meanings, they are also included. Note that some words may function as more than one part of speech, and that function may affect their meaning.

1. **derive** (di rīv) *v:* **1.** to obtain or receive from a source. **2.** to infer. **3.** to trace the origin of, as a word.

2. **extension** (ek sten´ shən) *n:* **1.** the act of spreading, stretching, or enlarging in length, time, or area. **2.** an addition. **3.** range or extent. **4.** an educational program that extends resources to other geographical sites. **5.** an extra part, as an additional telephone connected to a line.

3. **inevitably** (in ev´ ə tə blē) *adv:* unavoidably; not preventable.

4. **parallel** (par′ ə lel) *adj:* **1.** being an equal distance apart and never meeting. **2.** similar; having comparable parts.

5. **presumably** (pri zōōm′ əb lē) *adv:* reasonably assumed; taken for granted.

6. **probability** (prob ə bil′ ə tē) *n:* **1.** the state of being likely to happen or probably true. **2.** a number expressing the likelihood of a specific event to occur.

7. **prominent** (prom′ ə nənt) *adj:* **1.** projecting or jutting outward. **2.** noticeable or easily seen. **3.** widely known; distinguished.

8. **random** (ran′ dəm) *adj:* chance; at **random:** having no specific purpose or objective.

9. **simultaneously** (sī məl tān′ ē əs lē) *adv:* existing or happening at the same time.

10. **virtually** (vər′ chōō ə lē) *adv:* almost entirely; nearly; for all practical purposes.

Exercise 4: Choose from Multiple Meanings

Some of the words you are studying in this chapter have several meanings. In this exercise, first determine which word best completes each sentence. (You will use words more than once.) Then indicate the number of the meaning from the word list that helped you make your choice.

a. extension   b. probability   c. prominent   d. derive   e. parallel

____ 1. Malcolm hoped to _____ a substantial income from his real estate investments.

____ 2. The late comedian Jimmy Durante was always recognizable in cartoons because of his _____ nose.

____ 3. The rental cottage had few electrical outlets and no telephone jack to use for her _____ phone.

____ 4. In his first art class, Jake learned how to use the image of _____ railroad tracks to show perspective.

____ 5. Professor Douglas introduced the notion of _____ to the students in her statistics class by demonstrating with a deck of cards.

X _IC_ 6. Several students in the humanities department organized

_____   a lecture series that featured _____ speakers including authors and social scientists.

ICe 7. Individuals often make close friends through support groups because fellow members often find they have led

_____   _____ lives.

✓ _d_ 8. Linguists support the idea that many modern words

_____   _____ from classical languages.

✓ _a_ 9. After two seasons, the art gallery proved so popular that its

_____   owners added an _____ wing so they could accommodate more paintings and painters.

✓ _b_ 10. After suffering from an infection after knee surgery, Doug

_____   was assured that the _____ of contracting another one was very slim.

Exercise 5: Use the Word Correctly

The sentences below contain underlined words that you have studied. Indicate whether the words are used correctly (C) or incorrectly (I).

✓ _C_ 1. Each spring, the bureau of student services conducts a lottery for dorm rooms for the following year by picking numbers at <u>random</u>.

X _IC_ 2. Jason regularly failed to set his alarm, so, <u>inevitably</u>, he was late to work every day.

X _I I_ 3. Because of his <u>prominent</u> film and television roles, the actor was rarely recognized on the street by his fans.

X _O I_ 4. An <u>extension</u> of the date to apply for jobs caused prospective employees to miss the deadline.

X _C I_ 5. Samantha <u>derived</u> her possessions among her grand nieces when she moved to a nursing home.

X _IC_ 6. <u>Presumably</u>, everyone who was invited to the wedding responded by the week before.

✓ _C_ 7. On the morning of the snowstorm, <u>virtually</u> all of Vera's math students arrived late to class.

✓ I   8. Though he couldn't be considered good-looking, Steve had such a charming <u>probability</u> that he was never without a date.

✓ C   9. At the circus, Jamie found he could not watch the activities in all three rings <u>simultaneously</u>.

✓ C   10. The geometry teacher instructed her students to draw a figure with two pairs of <u>parallel</u> lines.

Exercise 6: Write Your Own Sentences

Write a sentence that uses each of the words you studied in this chapter in a way that indicates your understanding of the word's meaning.

1. _____

2. _____

3. _____

4. _____

5. _____

6. _____

7. _____

8. _____

9. _____

10. _____

CHAPTER 8

The words in this chapter are the last set of high-frequency words you will study. As in the previous chapters, you will recognize some of the words, but you may not be able to provide definitions for them. You may have come across some of these words in an academic context, such as *ratio* in math or *myth* in literature. Others you may be familiar with through daily experiences, as a *yield* sign on a roadway. Others, like *phenomenon* and *pathology*, will probably sound familiar, but you might have a hard time defining them without context.

Read the following passage through completely. Then return to the beginning and write your definition for each numbered and underlined word.

Hooked on Mysteries

Mystery novels fascinate Bill, and he finds them an agreeable (1) <u>alternative</u> to the financial reading his job requires. When he ends his day as a stockbroker, trying to earn the maximum (2) <u>revenue</u> for his clients, he relaxes with a beer and a book. His current favorite series features a clever female detective with a boyfriend who specializes in (3) <u>pathology</u>. Together, they solve many murders that were made to look like accidents. In fact, in the five books Bill has read about the pair, their success (4) <u>ratio</u> is 5:0. Max, the pathologist, often conducts autopsies that reveal clues indicating death did not occur from natural causes. Georgia, the detective, often takes the (5) <u>initiative</u> of involving Max before the police even suspect foul play. The author of the detective series perpetuates the (6) <u>myth</u> that the police are just amateurs who need the assistance of a Max and a Georgia. Whereas the police investigations (7) <u>yield</u> little in the way of results, the detective pair are able to explain the most bizarre (8) <u>phenomenon</u> with seemingly little effort. In the book Bill is currently reading, Georgia has a theory that a leak in a propane tank that released poisonous (9) <u>emissions</u> into the guest cottage of a movie star was not accidental. When Bill's friends tease him about his "addiction" to the books, he shrugs his shoulders in a (10) <u>gesture</u> that seems to indicate he doesn't plan to apologize for his literary taste.

Exercise 1: Define

Write your definition for each word as it is used in the passage.

1. alternative   *option, choice*
2. revenue   *money, earnings*
3. pathology   *study of disease*
4. ratio   *proportion*
5. initiative   *beginning, introductory step*
6. myth   *story, legend*
7. yield   *give up, give away*
8. phenomenon   *occurence, happening*

9. emissions *substance released / give off*

10. gesture *Body motion / hand motion*

Exercise 2: Match

Match the terms in Column A with their definitions in Column B.

Column A	Column B
1. ratio *e*	a. occurrence; happening
2. myth *c*	b. a substance released or given off
3. phenomenon *a*	c. legend; story
4. revenue *f*	d. hand or body motion
5. yield *i*	e. proportion; relationship
6. alternative *g*	f. money; earnings
7. pathology *j*	g. option; choice
8. emission *b*	h. introductory step
9. gesture *d*	i. give up; give way
10. initiative *h*	j. the study of disease

Exercise 3: Fill In

Fill in the letter of the word that best completes each sentence.

a. yield	d. gesture	g. revenue	i. initiative
b. pathology	e. alternative	h. ratio	j. phenomenon
c. myth	f. emissions		

_g_ 1. Caroline's failure to file her tax return on time resulted in

a fine, according to a notice from the Internal _____ Service.

_e_ 2. One feature of the college program that appealed to Jay

was the option of independent study as an _____ to a formal class.

_h_ 3. Marta was pleased by the _____ of two men to every woman at the dance.

_C **N**_   4. In the 1960s, feminists tried to dispel the _____ that men should be the breadwinners and women should stay at home.

_**X** j_   5. When he visited his daughter's first-grade class, John was amazed by the _____ of silence that descended when the teacher turned out the lights.

_b_   6. While in medical school, Sierra decided she would specialize in _____ .

_f_   7. Although _____ standards for automobiles vary from state to state, all are stricter than they used to be.

_a_   8. Failure to _____ to a pedestrian in a crosswalk cost Rick a $40 fine.

_i_   9. Praised for his _____ in handling an emergency situation in the subway, the patrolman received a medal from the mayor.

_d_   10. In a _____ of despair, Lois put her head on the table and sobbed.

WORD LIST

The following list gives dictionary-type definitions of the words you are studying in this chapter. Each entry includes the word's pronunciation and part of speech. If the word has multiple meanings, they are also included. Note that some words may function as more than one part of speech, and that function may affect their meaning.

1. **alternative** (ôl tər′ nə tiv) *n:* **1.** a choice between two or more things. *adj:* **2.** offering a choice: *an alternative program.*

2. **emission** (i mish′ ən) *n:* **1.** substances given off into the air. **2.** something discharged or given out. **3.** a verbal expression or utterance.

3. **gesture** (jes′ chər) *n:* **1.** a movement of the hands or body, often used for emphasis while speaking. **2.** something done as a formality or an indication of attitude: *a gesture of friendship.*

4. **initiative** (i nish′ ē ə tiv) *n:* **1.** the ability to begin or follow through with a plan. **2.** the action of beginning or starting; introductory step. **3.** the spirit needed to initiate action. **4.** a process by which laws can be enacted directly by a popular vote.

5. **myth** (mith) *n:* **1.** a traditional story that tells of gods and goddesses or tries to explain some natural phenomenon. **2.** any imaginary tale or story. **3.** a notion or belief based more on tradition or convenience than on fact.

6. **pathology** (pa thol′ ə jē) *n:* the scientific or medical study of the nature, causes, and symptoms of diseases.

7. **phenomenon** (fi nom′ ə non) *n:* **1.** any observable or visible occurrence, happening, or fact. **2.** any unusual fact or occurrence. **3.** an outward sign of the working out of a natural law. **4.** an extraordinary person.

8. **ratio** (rā′ shē ō) *n:* **1.** the relationship in number or degree of two numbers; rate. **2.** a mathematical quotient or fraction expressing the relative size of two quantities.

9. **revenue** (rev′ ə nyōo) *n:* **1.** total income of a government. **2.** yield or profit from property or investment.

10. **yield** (yēld) *v:* **1.** to give forth or produce: *yield fruit; yield a good crop.* **2.** to bring in, as a return on an investment. **3.** to relinquish or give up: *to yield territory to the enemy.* **4.** to give way. *n:* **5.** the amount yielded or produced. **6.** the profit from an investment.

Exercise 4: Choose from Multiple Meanings

Some of the words you are studying in this chapter have several meanings. In this exercise, first determine which word best completes each sentence. (You will use words more than once.) Then indicate the number of the meaning from the word list that helped you make your choice.

a. myth   b. yield   c. gesture   d. initiative   e. phenomenon

__c__   1. The photographer captured the children's _____ of hopelessness as they raised their empty bowls.
____

__e__   2. Chris Evert was considered quite a _____ in the world of tennis when she was quite young.
____

__d__   3. On his own _____, Perdit designed and implemented a new check-out procedure that significantly reduced customer waiting time.
____

__a__   4. Primitive people often used _____ to explain occurrences they didn't understand, like thunderstorms and lightning.
____

_C B_   5. As a _____ of hostility, the wrestler walked right by his opponent without even acknowledging his presence.

_b_   6. During the hearing on the budget amendment, the senator from New Jersey offered to _____ the floor to his colleague from Maine.

_b_   7. Favorable growing conditions, sunshine, and rain promised a record _____ for wheat farmers in the Midwest.

_a_   8. Educational research studies have disproved the _____ that day care deprives children of necessary experiences they would have had at home.

_e_   9. Molly was struck by the _____ that whenever she walked into her dorm everyone stopped talking.

_d_   10. When the manager failed to show up for work, Jim took the _____ to give his fellow employees their assignments for the day.

Exercise 5: Use the Word Correctly

The sentences below contain underlined words that you have studied. Indicate whether the words are used correctly (C) or incorrectly (I).

_I_   1. When he decided to study <u>pathology</u>, Peter realized many of his classes would focus on world history.

_I_   2. An early blizzard stranded the hikers in the mountains without enough <u>ratio</u> to last until help arrived.

_C_   3. A decline in the town's <u>revenue</u> plus the added expense of frequent snow removal meant several municipal workers would be laid off.

_C_   4. Lee inherited a thriving clothing business from his mother, but his lack of <u>initiative</u> caused its downfall.

_C_   5. Sophie felt she had no <u>alternative</u> to accepting a low-paying job since it was the only one she had been offered.

_I_   6. To treat Marcia's migraine headaches, her doctor prescribed two doses of <u>phenomenon</u> at bedtime.

✗ _I_   7. Craig's <u>emission</u> of guilt made the prosecutor's task an easy one.

_C_   8. As a <u>gesture</u> of hospitality, Omar invited his new neighbors for dinner.

_C_   9. Mai concluded that the discussion was useless when she realized her dinner companion would not <u>yield</u> a single point.

_C_   10. Loretta's favorite <u>myth</u> explained the origin of the seasons.

Exercise 6: Write Your Own Sentences

Write a sentence that uses each of the words you studied in this chapter in a way that indicates your understanding of the word's meaning.

1. _____

2. _____

3. _____

4. _____

5. _____

6. _____

7. _____

8. _____

9. _____

10. _____

CHAPTER 9

An *idiom* is an expression that cannot be understood by the meanings of its parts. For example, if someone said she had heard "a *blow by blow* description of a party," you couldn't figure out the meaning of the expression from defining the individual words. If you try to interpret the phrase literally, you may have an image of a party that ended up in a brawl. What the speaker actually means is she heard a very detailed account of the party. The origin of the idiom is from boxing, and it referred to a report of a fight in which every punch was described.

Many idiomatic expressions that native English speakers take for granted are very confusing for non-native speakers. Imagine the images that the following idioms can produce if taken literally:

He wanted to ask her out, but he got *cold feet*.
I'm *dying* to hear all about your job interview.
After complaining about the new boss's requests, her
    employees *fell into line*.
To pass my chemistry test, I'll have to *pull an all-nighter*.
When Paul returns from vacation, *fill him in on* what's happened.

Entire books and dictionaries of American idioms have been written to explain the meanings of some of the expressions we hear and read. In this chapter and the next, you will study a small sampling of American idioms. The idioms that are included were chosen because they are common, but not everyday expressions. You can expect to come across them in academic settings and in the workplace. Idioms that are frequently used in conversation, such as "*I'm through* with him *for good*," and "I *can't tell* if she's serious," have not been included. In some cases, related idioms or those that may be confused are grouped together. They are presented in context so you can get a sense of how they are used. In many cases, the idioms have multiple meanings. After you review them in context, check the definitions for all the meanings before you complete the exercise.

I. **bring out**
    bring around
    bring up

My colleagues had been talking about a new sales approach and I expected them to *bring it up* at the department meeting. Though our boss is reluctant to try new ideas, Charlene thought she could *bring him around*. When he arrived at the meeting, Mr. Cortines said he knew there were some controversial proposals under consideration and suggested we *bring them out in the open*.

Definitions:

a. **bring out:**   **1.** expose to the public. **2.** make a formal or social debut. **3.** introduce a new product or publish a book.

b. **bring around:**   **1.** bring someone to another's house to meet. **2.** help someone regain consciousness. **3.** persuade someone to agree.

c. **bring up:**   **1.** to mention a topic. **2.** to raise, as a child or protégé.

Exercise 1: Select the letter of the best idiomatic phrase to complete the sentences below.

_a_ 1. After she had been pulled out of the burning building, fire-fighters tried to bring Jessie _____ before carrying her to the ambulance.

_b_ 2. Though the tuition at his college of choice exceeded what his parents planned to spend, Mark felt sure he could bring them _____.

_c_ 3. Aunt Nancy agreed to bring _____ Samuel after his parents died in an automobile accident.

_b_ 4. As a result of the new campaign disclosure regulations, the newspaper reporter brought _____ a list of contributors.

_b_ 5. Martha hoped her father wouldn't bring _____ her speeding ticket at the family party.

II. **go with**
     go through

After listening to several suggestions, Mr. Cortines announced that he would *go through* all of the research reports and other relevant information before he made a decision about reorganizing the sales force according to product or location. After gathering much data and considering the opinions of several experts, he would decide which plan to *go with*.

Definitions:

a. **go through:**   **1.** fail to stop. **2.** review in detail. **3.** experience.

b. **go with:**   **1.** accompany or date. **2.** match, as in clothing.
                     3. choose.

Exercise 2: Select the letter of the best idiomatic phrase to complete the sentences below.

_a_   1. I spent an hour going _____ my closet and decided I have nothing to wear to the wedding.

_b_   2. Ernesto asked Anita if she would go _____ him to the dance.

_b_   3. Benazir was delighted to learn that the soft-drink manufacturer would go _____ her advertising firm.

_a_   4. The earthquake was the most devastating experience Charles had ever gone _____.

_b_   5. The shoes Sheila selected don't go _____ her dress at all.

III. **turn on**
      turn over
      turn in

At the meeting the following week, Mr. Cortines asked Charlene, Brad, Arturo, and Imelda to *turn in* their reports and recommendations. Each member of the committee had prepared a five-minute presentation ending with a recommendation. When Brad found himself in the minority, he *turned on* his colleagues and accused them of setting him up for failure. As the discussion deteriorated, Mr. Cortines asked the committee to *turn over* the task of summarizing their findings to him.

Definitions:

a. **turn on:**   **1.** to attack someone. **2.** to excite someone. **3.** to switch on, as a radio.

b. **turn in:**   **1.** to report someone for having done something bad. **2.** to submit a report. **3.** to return something, as a library book or a found object.

c. **turn over:**   **1.** to roll someone or something over. **2.** to deliver someone or something to a another.

Exercise 3: Select the letter of the best idiomatic phrase to complete the sentences below.

_____ 1. At the hotel's departure desk, Madeline paid her bill and turned _____ her key.

_____ 2. Anxious to see his latest movie, Beth confessed that Kevin Costner really turns her _____.

_____ 3. Juan picked up a wallet on a street corner and turned it _____ at the nearest police station.

_____ 4. An error message appeared on the screen because Harry had forgotten to turn _____ the printer when he started to work at the computer.

_____ 5. After living as a fugitive for 20 years, the bank robber turned herself _____ to the authorities.

IV.   **hold up**
      open up

Charlene and Imelda felt that Brad was *holding up* what they saw as a great step forward for the sales division. They were looking forward to assignments that allowed them to work only with products they knew all about. Brad, on the other hand, felt that the proposed reorganization would *open up* his territory to competition from members of his own company.

Definitions:

a. **hold up:**   1. to provide support.   2. rob.   3. delay or detain.   4. set up as an example or hero.

b. **open up:**   1. unwrap.   2. bring up for discussion.   3. present an opportunity.   4. start a business.   5. accelerate a vehicle. 6. remove a source of congestion.

Exercise 4:   Select the letter of the best idiomatic phrase to complete the sentences below.

_____   1. After class, the professor said to his students, "Please don't

_____ me up. I'm on my way to a meeting."

_____   2. Guy's most embarrassing moment at the surprise party

occurred when the guests insisted he _____ his gifts.

_____   3. Although the robber only used a toy gun to _____ the store, the clerk believed it was real.

_____   4. When jobs at the automobile factory _____, applicants line up the night before.

_____   5. After a month of delays in obtaining the necessary permits,

the new beauty shop was able to _____ on Saturday.

V.   **make up**
     wash up

Brad argued that his colleagues couldn't establish a rapport with his clients and that they wouldn't be able to find his customers. Even Mr. Cortines could see that Brad was *making up* one excuse after another. Though the others pointed out that he would be gaining just as much sales area as the others, Brad was convinced that if this plan went through, he would be *washed up* as a salesman.

Definitions:

a. **make up:**   **1.** to repay. **2.** lie or create fiction or poetry. **3.** mix or put together. **4.** apply makeup. **5.** mend a quarrel.

b. **wash up:**   **1.** to clean up. **2.** to carry up on the shore from the water. **3.** to end someone's career.

Exercise 5:   Select the letter of the best idiomatic phrase to complete the sentences below.

_____   1. Sally's job for the school play was to _____ all the actors before their first stage appearance.

_____   2. When the visiting nurse arrives, she said, "Let's start with a _____."

_____   3. The architect planned to _____ a model of the new school building to show to the board members.

_____   4. Roy hoped that when they returned home from work today, he and Lisa could _____.

_____   5. Remnants of the sunken ship continued to _____ on the beach for weeks after the storm.

VI. **at large**
     out of sight

Finally, after one more week of consideration, Mr. Cortines made his decision and unveiled the approved plan. Each of the sales representatives would serve as an expert *at large* for a specified number of products. The representatives were expected to work cooperatively, since each may be dealing with the same customers. Smiles appeared on the faces of Charlene, Imelda, and Arturo. Brad groaned inwardly but said nothing. When Mr. Cortines revealed the products assignments, he turned to Brad. "Since you are our most experienced and successful representative, I have assigned you to our three best-selling products." After he regained his composure, all Brad said was, "*Out of sight!* Thanks, Mr. Cortines."

Definitions:

a. **at large:**   **1.** free or uncaptured. **2.** in general. **3.** representing the whole group.

b. **out of sight:** **1.** not visible. **2.** very expensive. **3.** awesome.

Exercise 6: Select the letter of the best idiomatic phrase to complete the sentences below.

_____ 1. After seeing her son off to college, Leila watched the airplane until it was _____.

_____ 2. The students elected one representative per class and four representatives _____ to the student council.

_____ 3. Two weeks after the prison break, three dangerous criminals were still _____.

_____ 4. Rosaria enjoyed the fashion show until she consulted her program and learned that the prices were _____.

_____ 5. As he opened the envelope that contained front-row tickets to the concert, Erik yelled, "_____."

CHAPTER 10

Quite a few idioms are also considered clichés. A *cliché* (klē shā′) is an overused expression that, as a result, carries little meaning. Some examples include:

She's *always there for me.*
He packed *everything but the kitchen sink.*
She *missed* that shot *by a mile.*
I mean it *from the bottom of my heart.*

Although figurative language can enhance your writing and speaking, clichés usually detract from its quality. You may use figurative language effectively when you are writing description. For example, you may recall reading a passage in which an author compared a child's blond hair to corn silk. This comparison may help you to visualize the character. On the other hand, rather than saying, "He packed everything but the kitchen sink," consider this alternative: "Randy's Volkswagen nearly burst with all his possessions. His clothes and books took up most of the back seat, and his TV and toaster were beside him."

As you work through the idioms in this chapter, you will not meet clichés. They are not included here because they are so common that most people are familiar with them. They also lend little information to a conversation or piece of writing.

I. **put up**
    put down

As Sue and Janice were *putting up* decorations for the Valentine's dance, they talked about Alex, their friend Lisa's ex-boyfriend. Although the young women were generally fair and generous in their opinions of others, they had no qualms about *putting* Alex *down*.

Definitions:

a. **put up:**   **1.** raise. **2.** provide a room or bed. **3.** preserve or can food. **4.** offer an idea for consideration. **5.** prepare a meal to go. **6.** recommend a candidate. **7.** construct a building. **8.** provide money. **9.** set one's hair. **10.** prepare to fight.

b. **put down:**   **1.** criticize or belittle. **2.** write something. **3.** crush or end an uprising. **4.** land an airplane. **5.** pay, as a deposit

Exercise 1: Select the letter of the best idiomatic phrase to complete each sentence below.

_____   1. Let me _____ you _____ for two tickets to the concert, and you can pay me later.

_____   2. Angela _____ 25 quarts of tomatoes last August.

_____   3. Amparah arranged an affordable mortgage payment because she _____ $10,000 when she bought her house.

_____   4. After two hours of circling the field, the pilot was finally able to _____ the plane _____ in Chicago.

_____   5. When the guest coaches arrived to work with the soccer team, parents of the players offered to _____ them _____ for the week.

> II. **check out**
> **pick up**
>
> After a lunch break, Sue and Janice returned to the gym and continued with their preparations. While they were working, other students came by to *check out* their progress. They declined most offers of help, but they gladly accepted when Jerry volunteered to give the place a final sweep and to *pick up* any trash that was left around.

Definitions:

a. **check out:**   1. inspect. 2. record someone's departure, as from a hotel. 3. record a loan of something. 4. determine the truth.

b. **pick up:**   1. lift. 2. take on a passenger while driving. 3. give a ride to a hitchhiker. 4. meet someone at a bar. 5. arrest. 6. clean a room. 7. purchase something. 8. learn something. 9. increase the tempo of music. 10. resume something. 11. receive radio or TV signals. 12. find a trail.

Exercise 2: Select the letter of the best idiomatic phrase to complete each sentence below.

_____ 1. I'd like to _____ the new restaurant that opened in town.

_____ 2. You can _____ the books on this shelf for two weeks.

_____ 3. While vacationing in Mexico, Ellen was able to _____ a little Spanish.

_____ 4. On some state highways, it is illegal to _____ a hitchhiker.

_____ 5. Although we had to _____ of our room by 10:00, the hotel provided a courtesy suite so we could shower and change before our flight.

III.   **straighten up**
        set up

By 6:00 the gym was decorated and completely *straightened up*. Just before Sue, Janice, and Jerry left to eat dinner and change, the members of the band arrived to *set up* their equipment.

Definitions:

a. **straighten up:**   **1.** stand something upright. **2.** clean up.
                          3. stand straighter. **4.** behave better.

b. **set up:**   **1.** lie to someone or get them in trouble. **2.** put in an upright position. **3.** assemble. **4.** establish or arrange. **5.** plan. **6.** make drinks.

Exercise 3: Select the letter of the best idiomatic phrase to complete each sentence below.

_____ 1. After teaching for 25 years, Miss Gray still insists that her

students _____ in their seats before she begins a lesson.

_____ 2. One of Pam's jobs as an administrative assistant to the

president is to _____ conferences that include meals and guest speakers.

_____ 3. When Joe realized he had been seated next to the only single

woman at the dinner, he thought he had been _____ as her escort for the evening.

_____ 4. Charles's dad hoped that his time in the army would help

him to _____ .

_____ 5. After the storm, Paul needed to _____ the flagpole that had been battered by the heavy winds.

IV.   **fall apart**
      fall in line
      fall through

A sudden thunderstorm caused a power failure just before the dance was about to start. After all the effort, Sue couldn't believe everything could *fall apart* so quickly. She felt disappointment about a possible cancellation. In addition, the profits were designated for a local day care project. She would hate to have her promise of a substantial donation *fall through*. When the other members of the committee arrived, Janice adopted a positive attitude and began to see how she could work things out. With Janice as an example, the rest of the group *fell into line* and searched for candles and a portable generator.

Definitions:

a. **fall apart:**   **1.** to break into pieces or become unworkable. **2.** to disband. **3.** to become disorganized or disoriented.

b. **fall in line:**   **1.** to line up one after the other. **2.** to behave as expected or as others do. **3.** to agree to another's point of view.

c. **fall through:**   to not happen.

Exercise 4: Select the letter of the best idiomatic phrase to complete each sentence below.

_____   1. When he lost his job, Matt's plans to buy a house and start a family _____.

_____   2. Akesha had a full weekend planned, but when the rain started, all arrangements for outdoor activities _____.

_____   3. Within six months, any salesperson who had not learned to _____with company policy about dress and customer service was fired.

_____   4. A retired military officer, Mr. Marchesi expected his first year biology students to _____ quickly and efficiently.

_____   5. After one washing, the dress shirt Marty had bought on sale _____.

V. **keep back**
   work on

At 8:00, when the first group arrived to buy tickets, the back-up arrangements were almost complete. Chico's job was to *keep the crowd back* as his friends helped the band hook up their equipment to the portable power source. The repair crew from the electric company continued to *work on* repairing the wires, and by 8:30, the lights were back on and the band members urged everyone to get out on the dance floor.

Definitions:

a. **keep back:** **1.** prevent any movement forward. **2.** retain in school. **3.** to keep a secret. **4.** to make something unavailable.

b. **work on:** **1.** to repair or build. **2.** to try to persuade. **3.** to treat medically.

Exercise 5: Select the letter of the best idiomatic phrase to complete each sentence below.

_____ 1. Sam's teacher convinced his mother that her decision to

_____ him _____ for another year of kindergarten was in his best interest.

_____ 2. Rachel planned to _____ her father to buy her a new car as a graduation present.

_____ 3. Frank decided to _____ the news that his grandfather had died until Drew finished taking his exams.

_____ 4. Tom _____ the kitchen faucet until the hot water no longer surged out.

_____ 5. For the final clearance sale, the store manager hired additional guards to _____ the crowds and allow a limited number in the store at a time.

> VI. **call the shots**
>   **call** someone's **bluff**
>   **call** someone **on the carpet**
>
> At 8:45, Mr. Tedesco, the faculty chaperone, arrived at the dance. He was about to apologize for being late when he saw all the candles and the portable generator. Bursting with anger, he went looking for Sue to *call her on the carpet* for creating a fire hazard. He ranted and raved about the committee's lack of judgment and threatened to cancel the dance immediately and send everyone home. Chico decided to *call his bluff*. He encouraged Mr. Tedesco to take the microphone and announce a cancellation. He also mentioned that Mr. T. would be responsible for refunding the tickets and paying the band. In addition, he felt sure the principal would be interested in the reason the chaperone arrived forty-five minutes after the dance started. And who would tell the daycare center that there would be no donation? Mr. T. realized he had lost the battle and agreed that Chico, Sue, and Janice could *call the shots* in their report to the principal. In the meantime, all agreed to stow the generator, pack up the candles, and enjoy the rest of the evening.

Definitions:

a. **call the shots:**   make decisions; take charge.

b. **call** someone's **bluff:**   to challenge someone to do what he or she threatens; to demand proof of a claim.

c. **call** someone **on the carpet:** to criticize or reprimand.

Exercise 6: Select the letter of the best idiomatic phrase to complete each sentence below.

_____ 1. Mr. Goodyear, the physical education teacher, claimed he could do 75 push-ups until his fifth grade students

  _____.

_____ 2. Since David brought essentially all the capital to the business

  partnership, he felt entitled to _____.

_____ 3. After a difficult encounter with the parent of a student, the tennis club manager _____ the young instructor _____ for rudeness.

_____ 4. When the Seahawks had a 21–0 lead, the coach gave the quarterback permission to _____ on the field.

_____ 5. After years of his threatening to leave her, Zoe _____ her husband's _____ and packed his suitcase for him.

ANSWERS TO EXERCISES

CHAPTER 1

Check your answers for the exercises in Chapter 1.

Exercise 1 - Definitions

(Student answers will vary.) The definitions provided here are simpler than the dictionary-type definitions included in the word list.

1. frequently: often; many times
2. established: set up; started
3. determine: find out
4. capital: money; funds
5. significant: important; meaningful
6. campaign: special effort to raise money; fund-raiser
7. effective: useful; successful
8. indicated: said; showed; let people know
9. requirements: necessities; criteria; conditions
10. circumstances: situation; condition

Exercise 2 - Match

1. g   6. f
2. d   7. c
3. h   8. a
4. i   9. b
5. j   10. e

Exercise 3 - Fill-In

1. b   6. h
2. d   7. j
3. e   8. i
4. c   9. g
5. a   10. f

Exercise 4 - Multiple Meanings

1. b 1   6. d 1
2. c 3   7. a 3
3. d 3   8. c 2
4. c 1   9. a 1
5. b 4   10. d 4

Exercise 5 - Use Word Correctly

1. I   6. C
2. C   7. I
3. C   8. C
4. I   9. C
5. C   10. C

Exercise 6 - Accept reasonable student sentences.

CHAPTER 2

Check your answers for the exercises in Chapter 2.

Exercise1 - Definitions

(Student answers will vary.) The definitions provided here are simpler than the dictionary-type definitions included in the word list.

1. traditional: accepted, customary

2. literary: related to literature or reading

3. recognized: remembered someone or something from before

4. expression: communication through words, gestures, or facial appearance

5. sanctions: penalties or punishing restrictions

6. phase: stage or period

7. providence: care

8. nevertheless: in spite of, but

9. vocational: related to job training

10. initial: at first

Exercise 2 - Match

1. c	6. h
2. d	7. f
3. e	8. b
4. j	9. g
5. i	10. a

Exercise 3 - Fill-In

1. e	6. i
2. g	7. d
3. j	8. b
4. c	9. f
5. h	10. a

Exercise 4 - Multiple Meanings

1. b 3	6. e 1
2. c 2	7. a 5
3. a 4	8. e 3
4. d 3	9. d 1
5. b 1	10. c 3

Exercise 5 - Use Word Correctly

1. I	6. C
2. C	7. C
3. C	8. C
4. I	9. I
5. I	10. C

Exercise 6 - Accept reasonable student sentences.

CHAPTER 3

Check your answers for the exercises in Chapter 3.

Exercise 1 - Definitions

(Student answers will vary.) The definitions provided here are simpler than the dictionary-type definitions included in the word list.

1. capable: able; qualified; prepared
2. contemporary: someone the same age; peer; modern
3. procedure: way to do something; routine
4. commercial: related to business or making money
5. substantial: a lot; significant; large
6. maintenance: taking care of something; upkeep
7. commerce: trade, business
8. potential: power; capability; what you can become
9. groomed: cleaned-up; presentable
10. apparent: as it seemed; what it looked like

Exercise 2 - Match

1. j	6. c
2. d	7. h
3. g	8. a
4. f	9. b
5. e	10. i

Exercise 3 - Fill-In

1. b	6. i
2. c	7. f
3. h	8. e
4. g	9. a
5. d	10. j

Exercise 4 - Multiple Meanings

1. e 2	6. b 4
2. a 3	7. a 2
3. c 4	8. c 3
4. d 2	9. d 1
5. e 3	10. b 5

Exercise 5 - Use Word Correctly

1. C	6. I
2. C	7. C
3. I	8. C
4. I	9. I
5. C	10. C

Exercise 6 - Accept reasonable student sentences.

CHAPTER 4

Check your answers for the exercises in Chapter 4.

Exercise 1 - Definitions

(Student answers will vary.) The definitions provided here are simpler than the dictionary-type definitions included in the word list.

1. interpretation: one's point of view or analysis
2. generation: group of people in the same age group
3. entitled: having a right to something
4. intensity: concentration; force
5. vital: very important
6. wage: salary; earnings
7. welfare: a social program that takes care of poor people
8. conventional: acceptable; traditional
9. components: parts
10. minute: 60 seconds

Exercise 2 - Match

1. f
2. h
3. e
4. g
5. c
6. a
7. i
8. b
9. j
10. d

Exercise 3 - Fill-In

1. i
2. d
3. g
4. e
5. j
6. c
7. a
8. b
9. h
10. f

Exercise 4 - Multiple Meanings

1. d 1
2. e 2
3. c 4
4. b 1
5. d 2
6. a 4
7. b 2
8. e 1
9. c 1
10. a 1

Exercise 5 - Use Word Correctly

1. C
2. I
3. C
4. C
5. C
6. I
7. C
8. I
9. I
10. C

Exercise 6 - Accept reasonable student sentences.

CHAPTER 5

Check your answers for the exercises in Chapter 5.

Exercise 1 - Definitions

(Student answers will vary.) The definitions provided here are simpler than the dictionary-type definitions included in the word list.

1. integration: the process of bringing together different groups
2. recognition: the realization that you know someone or something
3. mere: only, as in a mere $4
4. testimony: formal statements
5. chamber: room
6. precision: care, accuracy, exactness
7. burden: chore, load
8. expenditures: costs, bills to be paid
9. provision: a restriction or specified qualification
10. accomplish: achieve, be successful at

Exercise 2 - Match

1. d	6. a
2. f	7. b
3. h	8. e
4. j	9. c
5. i	10. g

Exercise 3 - Fill-In

1. c	6. f
2. j	7. e
3. b	8. g
4. i	9. h
5. d	10. a

Exercise 4 - Multiple Meanings

1. b	1	6. c	4
2. e	2	7. b	2
3. a	4	8. e	1
4. c	1, 2, or 3	9. a	5
5. d	1	10. d	2

Exercise 5 - Use Word Correctly

1. C	6. C
2. I	7. C
3. C	8. I
4. I	9. C
5. I	10. C

Exercise 6 - Accept reasonable student sentences.

CHAPTER 6

Check your answers for the exercises in Chapter 6.

Exercise 1 - Definitions

(Student answers will vary.) The definitions provided here are simpler than the dictionary-type definitions included in the word list.

1. distinction: honor or excellence
2. external: outside
3. bureau: department
4. editorial: newspaper article with an opinion
5. vice: bad habit; evil or illegal acts
6. excess: more than
7. varied: ranged, changed
8. assumption: something believed before it is proved
9. investment: something (money, time, etc.) committed for future gain
10. identification: the act of pointing out or recognizing someone

Exercise 2 - Match

1. e   6. a
2. g   7. i
3. f   8. d
4. j   9. h
5. c   10. b

Exercise 3 - Fill-In

1. e   6. b
2. c   7. h
3. g   8. a
4. d   9. i
5. j   10. f

Exercise 4 - Multiple Meanings

1. d 1   6. c 1
2. b 2   7. e 5
3. c 3   8. d 2 or 3
4. e 1 or 2   9. b 1
5. a 2   10. a 1

Exercise 5 - Use Word Correctly

1. I   6. C
2. C   7. I
3. I   8. C
4. I   9. C
5. C   10. C

Exercise 6 - Accept reasonable student sentences.

CHAPTER 7

Check your answers for the exercises in Chapter 7.

Exercise 1 - Definitions

(Student answers will vary.) The definitions provided here are simpler than the dictionary-type definitions included in the word list.

1. virtually: almost; essentially
2. random: chance; unplanned
3. parallel: similar; lined up at a distance apart
4. prominent: noticeable
5. presumably: probably
6. probability: likelihood
7. simultaneously: at the same time
8. derived: came from
9. inevitably: bound to happen
10. extension: later time period

Exercise 2 - Match

1. i	6. e
2. j	7. f
3. h	8. a
4. d	9. c
5. b	10. g

Exercise 3 - Fill-In

1. i	6. h
2. f	7. a
3. c	8. e
4. g	9. j
5. d	10. b

Exercise 4 - Multiple Meanings

1. d 1	6. c 3
2. c 1	7. e 2
3. a 5	8. d 1 or 3
4. e 1	9. a 2
5. b 2	10. b 1

Exercise 5 - Use Word Correctly

1. C	6. C
2. C	7. C
3. I	8. I
4. I	9. C
5. I	10. C

Exercise 6 - Accept reasonable student sentences.

CHAPTER 8

Check your answers for the exercises in Chapter 8.

Exercise 1 - Definitions

(Student answers will vary.) The definitions provided here are simpler than the dictionary-type definitions included in the word list.

1. alternative: option, choice
2. revenue: money, income
3. pathology: the study of disease
4. ratio: proportion
5. initiative: gumption; assertiveness
6. myth: story, legend
7. yield: give way
8. phenomenon: happening
9. emissions: something discharged or given out
10. gesture: hand motion

Exercise 2 - Match

1. e	6. g
2. c	7. j
3. a	8. b
4. f	9. d
5. i	10. h

Exercise 3 - Fill-In

1. g	6. b
2. e	7. f
3. h	8. a
4. c	9. i
5. j	10. d

Exercise 4 - Multiple Meanings

1. c	1	6. b 4
2. e	4	7. b 5
3. d	1 or 2	8. a 3
4. a	1	9. e 2 or 1
5. c	2	10. d 3

Exercise 5 - Use Word Correctly

1. I	6. I
2. I	7. I
3. C	8. C
4. C	9. C
5. C	10. C

Exercise 6 - Accept reasonable student sentences.

CHAPTER 9

Check your answers for the exercises in Chapter 9.

Exercise 1

1. b
2. b
3. c
4. a
5. c

Exercise 2

1. a
2. b
3. b
4. a
5. b

Exercise 3

1. b or c
2. a
3. b or c
4. a
5. b

Exercise 4

1. a
2. b
3. a
4. b
5. b

Exercise 5

1. a
2. b
3. a
4. a
5. b

Exercise 6

1. b
2. a
3. a
4. b
5. b

CHAPTER 10

Check your answers for the exercises in Chapter 10.

Exercise 1

1. b
2. a
3. b
4. b
5. a

Exercise 2

1. a
2. a
3. b
4. b
5. a

Exercise 3

1. a
2. b
3. b
4. a
5. a

Exercise 4

1. a or c
2. a or c
3. b
4. b
5. a

Exercise 5

1. a
2. b
3. a
4. b
5. a

Exercise 6

1. b
2. a
3. c
4. a
5. b

BIBLIOGRAPHY

Dahl, Hartvig. *Word Frequencies of Spoken American English.* Essex, Conn.: Verbatim, 1979.

Kucera H. and Francis, W. N. *Computational Analysis of Present-Day American English.* Providence, R.I.: Brown University Press, 1967.

Dictionaries consulted in creating this text include the following:

Merriam-Webster, Inc. *The Merriam Webster Dictionary.* Springfield, Mass.: Merriam-Webster, Inc., 1994.

Random House *Webster's College Dictionary.* New York: Random House, 1991.

Davies, Peter, ed. *The American Heritage Dictionary of the English Language.* Paperback edition. New York: Dell Publishing Co., 1980.

Funk & Wagnalls. *Funk & Wagnalls Standard Dictionary.* New York: Harper-Collins, 1980.